THE CATHOLIC UNIVERSITY OF AMERICA

STUDIES IN ROMANCE LANGUAGES AND LITERATURES

VOLUME LV

Frey, John Andrew

MOTIF SYMBOLISM

AMS PRESS
NEW YORK

COPYRIGHT, 1957 BY
THE CATHOLIC UNIVERSITY OF AMERICA

Reprinted with the permission of
The Catholic University of America
From the edition of 1957, Washington, D.C.
First AMS EDITION published 1969
Manufactured in the United States of America

Library of Congress Catalogue Card Number: 73-94193

AMS PRESS, INC.
New York, N.Y. 10003

MOTIF SYMBOLISM IN
THE DISCIPLES OF MALLARMÉ

MOTIF SYMBOLISM IN
THE DISCIPLES OF MALLARMÉ

BY
JOHN ANDREW FREY

THE CATHOLIC UNIVERSITY OF AMERICA PRESS
WASHINGTON, D.C.
1957

TO
MY MOTHER AND FATHER

TABLE OF CONTENTS

INTRODUCTION

The evolution of poetic purpose and form was so radical in the nineteenth century that it not only created a separation between the artist and the audience, but for those properly concerned with such matters, the literary historian, the critic, and the esthetician, the phenomenon of modern poetry is not yet quite understood except in its fragments. The lyric expansion of the Romantics was an initial and major development, for it not only enkindled a poetic which had been dead for almost two centuries, but produced a truly modern lyric sensibility which, in view of later innovations, was in its own right a true angoisse. The Parnassian threat to poetry was a temporary setback, something inevitable under the impact of the realistic epoch of which it was a curious accompaniment. The advent of Baudelaire reestablished a tradition, made important and startling innovations, and inaugurated modern poetry. The brief appearance of Rimbaud was the first major effort in the direction of a non-reasoned poetry, and with the work of Mallarmé, discursive reason as a poetic element seemed eliminated and modern poetry as we think of it today was established.

Because modern poetry is for the most part very difficult, serious critical and scholarly inquiry has been directed not only at individual poems, but intense examination has been made into the actual nature of the poetic act. The Symbolist poets commence this inquiry, and not long after them the Abbé Bremond[1] was among the first to state that a poem does not have to have a logical, in the sense of subject-predicate relationship, construction. Since the time of Bremond similar ideas have received such widespread approval that it makes it easy to accept the thesis of J. Krafft

---

[1] Henri Bremond, La Poésie pure (Paris, 1926).

ix

when he states: "L'examen objectif montre que les
grands vers français sont rarement beaux pour la seule
raison de l'idée pure...."[2]
Historical considerations of the role of the
poet and his place in society elucidate the problem
somewhat. Across the nineteenth century, the poet,
as Bornecque points out[3], retreats more and more into
an ivory tower of separation from the public. At the
end of the century not only is the poet in isolation,
but his work is no longer comprehensible to the average
reader. Here is a difficult problem. Admitting a
relationship between the life estrangement of the poet
in the face of a rising materialism, and the blossoming
of a positive, modern concept of poetry, we nevertheless
find this too facile and exterior an explanation. The
leap from an idealism which is in most instances a
social protest and which produces a work characterized
by an escapism (Romanticism), to an idealistic poetry
indifferent to society, and metaphysical in implication
(Mallarmé) is too great to be explained exclusively as
a quasi-spiritual reaction to a philistine society.
If so, we could not explain the essential differences
between Baudelaire and Mallarmé, for example.
Many critics place emphasis on an evaluation
of the poetic act itself, and it is in the light of
such appraisals that any historical consideration gains
merit. Reverdy, for example, states that it is the
poet's vision of the universe which distinguishes poetry
from the work of the scientist or the philosopher.
"Le propre du poète est de penser et de se penser en
images...."[4] Johansen says the same thing when he writes

[2]Jacques Krafft, La Forme et l'idée en poésie.
(Paris, 1944), p. 163.

[3]Jacques Bornecque, "Rêves et réalités du
Symbolisme," Revue des sciences humaines, No. 77
(January-March, 1955), pp. 5-23.

[4]Pierre Reverdy, "La Fonction poétique,"
Mercure de France, CCCVIII (1950), pp. 584-585.

that the order of poetic creation is image and then thought, and not vice-versa.[5] He goes on to state that nineteenth century poetry tried to reorder its vision in order to express a reality which the discursive reason could never convey. He thus defines Symbolism as a movement of pure poetry through images.[6]

We are in agreement with the definition of poetry which such arguments seem to imply. The Mellon Art Gallery Lectures of Jacques Maritain appear to give philosophical backing to these ideas for Maritain states that modern art has made an effort to free itself from nature and its forms, for through this deformation can be revealed "...a deeper reality, more akin to our dreams, angers, anguish, or melancholy...."[7] That is, there are sources of knowledge other than the discursive faculties, and it is to this other faculty, the intuition, or global apprehension, that modern art has turned. "In other words there is not only logical reason, but also, and prior to it, intuitive reason."[8]

Symbolism as a movement of pure poetry through images, the definition of Johansen, can be seen in embryo in the correspondance theory of Baudelaire. This concept gave impetus to the image to purify itself by the unifying force of synesthesia.[9] Correspondance directs poetry away from the arbitrary choice of terms which can be made by the discursive reason. There is no free choice in the selection of the simile or the metaphor. A rapport fatal as it was called by Flaubert, independent of the poet, must

---

[5]Svend Johansen, Le Symbolisme (Copenhagen, 1945), pp. 74-75.

[6]Ibid., p. 362.

[7]Jacques Maritain, Creative Intuition in Art and Poetry (New York, 1953), p. 73.

[8]Ibid., p. 75.

[9]See Marc Eigeldinger, L'Evolution dynamique de l'image (Neuchâtel, 1943), p. 123.

be achieved, one drawn from the sea of analogies to
be found in nature, a rapport which is not based on
the whim of the poet, but only on his sensibility as
a link in the universal unity, and his language as
the instrument for expressing this discovery, which
without the verbal power of the poet cannot be made.
Correspondance insists that there is not just a like-
ness between things, but a unity resulting from the
intermingling of all life. And as Fiser points out,
it is chance which leads to the discovery of this
unity between the interior and the exterior life.[10]
Inspiration can be explained in these terms as can the
obsession of Mallarmé with the démon de l'analogie.
The subjectivity of the poet is necessary but only
effective to the degree that he is aware of a true
correspondance. Such a subjectivity demands a strong
discipline in order to prohibit non-analogical imagery.
Correspondance thus sets poetry on the road to becoming
conscious of itself as distinct from prose creation,
and puts in motion a theory of unity which eventually
has drastic effects upon the traditional concept of
the image. Mallarmé's synthetic condensation is the
logical development of correspondance.
    Verlaine's literary Impressionism also gives
new direction and unity to the image, for while on one
side Impressionism becomes involved with a deterministic
Naturalism, at the same time, in poetry, it advances
the work started by Baudelaire. Hatzfeld's definition
of literary Impressionism, with Verlaine's Art poétique
as point of reference, as primacy of atmosphere, unconscious transfiguration, impressions of plein air,
refined response to nature, concentration on the
nuance, effacing of contours, no logically constructed
sentences, shading, metaphors rather than similes, the
suppression of single, discursive elements, perspective

---

[10]E. Fiser, Le Symbole littéraire (Paris,
no date given), p. 133.

by vague expressions, generally effected by the nominal
style without clarifying verbs[11], more than sufficiently
qualifies the work of Verlaine, shows the relation between Impressionism and Symbolism, and provides us with
a point of reference to be used in the body of this
text when we consider the proximity to Mallarmé and
Verlaine of some of the secondary Symbolist poets.

Rimbaud's legacy is the complete liberation
of poetry from reason. His déréglement des sens and
his concept of the poet as voyant conclude the Baudelairian essay. Like Mallarmé he makes stylistic innovations which preclude the primary appearance of
thought, and allow the image to act independently and
autonomously. Further, as Gengoux states, both Mallarmé
and Rimbaud are driven to a condensed poetic form because of an innate desire for unity.[12] The point of
contact then between the two poets would be a common
disregard for the discursive faculty as a sufficient
means of expression, and an analogical concept of the
universe which makes them strive for a poetry characterized by its elliptic and condensed form. Mallarmé
chooses symbols which can be considered as interior ones,
rooms, fans, gardens, while Rimbaud chooses his symbols
from active life, the revolution and the commune. Stylis-
tically this means for Mallarmé the suppression of the
verb to the profit of the substantive, the singular over
the plural, and a preference for the abstract. For
Rimbaud it means a preference for the verb, a pronounced
use of plurals, and a marked tense relationship.[13]

---

[11]Helmut Hatzfeld, Literature Through Art
(New York, 1952), p. 169.

[12]Jacques Gengoux, Le Symbolisme de Mallarmé
(Paris, 1950), p. 241.

[13]Ibid., pp. 241-242.

The unity of Rimbaud, therefore, it seems,
is more exterior and hence less potent than that of
Mallarmé. This is an important distinction to be
made between the processes of the two poets, and for
Johansen marks the distinction between a truly symbolic
poem and one that is not so. He writes concerning the
Bateau ivre:

> Il est symboliste du fait que ses
> images sont entièrement autonomes....
> De l'autre côté, il se distingue des
> vrais poèmes symbolistes du fait que
> ses images n'établissent pas de rapports.[14]

Mallarmé seems quite out of any ostentatious
poetic tradition at least as it evolved in the nineteenth century. In contrast with the Romantics,
Baudelaire, Rimbaud, and Verlaine, he is almost
bourgeois. Yet his poetry is the most radical of them
all.

His vocabulary is not characterized by word
creation or by an esoteric return to an earlier French
as is the case with Jean Moréas. He hardly experimented
with new devices as did Ghil, Kahn, and Vielé-Griffin,
for despite such a major exception as Un Coup de dés,
the alexandrine is his most usual line, and the sonnet
his characteristic form.

What is new with him is an elliptic and condensed manner of expression, a hermetic structure
which is the result of his analogical rather than
conceptual vision of life. Not only does Mallarmé
see the world as composed of interlocking analogies
(correspondance), but he conceives of them as so
joined as to be inseparable. Thus he works toward a
symbolization which will express in ambiguous terms
the oneness and paradox of existence. Maritain's
comments that the so-called difficult poem seems

---

[14] Johansen, op. cit., p. 292.

obscure either because of the "...heavy concentrated
intelligibility and the complexity of logical conno-
tations with which they are burdened...." or because
of such a concern for the significance of the logos
that there is a desire to make "...the whole fabric
of the poem one single intelligible word."[15] aptly
describe the position of Mallarmé.

Mallarmé's remarks on the dance indicate
that he so regarded artistic creation[16], and a whole
line of critics has been inclined to so regard his
work.[17] That is, appraisals of the poetic structure
of Mallarmé have shown a reduction and concentration
of the terms of the analogy to their essence from
which the symbol arises, pure, harmonious, and ambiguous.

No critic, in our opinion, has quite so well
defined the poetry of Mallarmé as Svend Johansen, whose
style inquiry we have already mentioned. Johansen
begins with a basic assumption which is inherent but
not explicit in other critical works on Symbolism.
Primary to all other considerations is what Johansen
calls the poet's "croyance au symbole," the belief
that the image, without the intrusion of thought can

---

[15]Maritain, op. cit., p. 261.

[16]See Stéphane Mallarmé, Oeuvres complètes
(Paris, 1945), p. 304.

[17]See Albert Mockel, Stéphane Mallarmé, un
Héros (Paris, 1899), p. 52, Etienne Bellot, Notes sur
le Symbolisme (Paris, 1908), p. 38, Albert Thibaudet,
La Poésie de Mallarmé (Paris, 1929), p. 92, Deborah
Aish, La Métaphore dans l'oeuvre de Mallarmé (Paris,
1938), p. 189, Pierre Beausire, Mallarmé, poésie et
poétique (Mermod, 1949), p. 176, Guy Delfel, L'Esthé-
tique de Mallarmé (Paris, 1951), p. 202, Jacques
Scherer, L'Expression littéraire dans l'oeuvre de
Mallarmé (Paris, 1947), p. 181, and Emilie Noulet,
Dix poèmes de Mallarmé (Geneva, 1949), p. 101.

be effective to produce a symbolization. This definition is an acceptable stylistic marking of the Symbolist concept of the image.

Johansen characterizes the two principal types of poetic function as symbole-thème and symbole-motif. In the first case, characteristic of Baudelaire, the symbolization is a result of the interaction of two or more images, which are of different value and are independent, and which interact to form a poetic tonality.[18] The other category, Motif Symbolism, is a function by which two images of equal value enjoy an interior correspondence, and are so joined as to make the tonality possible only because of their interpenetration and unity.[19] As Johansen writes: "En réalité, il n'est donc question d'une seule image, mais d'une image métamorphosée."[20]

To the latter category belongs the work of Mallarmé, and it is to him that Johansen looks for most of his examples. The Motif Symbolism of Mallarmé means a poetic style in which the craving for unity has reached the peak of expression. No term can be wasted; hence Mallarmé's patient reworking of each poem. No discursive element can be allowed to intrude; hence the extreme hermetic structure. Thus the labors of Mallarmé were directed toward a poetic creation in which each particle would be so constructed as to be inseparable from its neighbor, to produce a poetic whole in which the elements would be distinguishable, but inseparable.

Johansen's explanation of Surgi de la croupe et du bond most clearly illustrates the motif characteristics of the Mallarméan poem, the inability to achieve a poetic tonality without this interdependence of the image. Here is a pertinent passage from Johansen:

---

[18]Johansen, op. cit., pp. 85-86.

[19]Ibid.   [20]Ibid.

> Dans les tercets, il est donné la preuve
> la plus éclatante de l'identité des deux
> images symboliques, les deux solutions à
> cette accablant problème, la fleur et la
> sylphe. Le vase réapparaît; c'est sa
> croupe stérile et vide qui refuse de faire
> paraître une rose dans l'obscurité, une
> rose qui serait en même temps le baiser
> qui donnerait la vie à la sylphe ("naïf
> baiser des plus funèbres"; "funèbre"
> parce qu'elle romprait la stérilité du
> "pur vase"). En d'autres mots, les deux
> images symboliques sont fusionnées parce
> qu'elles sont toutes deux nées du même
> "prétexte", le vase, qui a sûrement été
> réel. Ce sont deux images de la même
> tonalité, séparées dans l'espace, mais
> se superposant dans le temps. [21]

Ambiguity is a characteristic feature of Motif
Symbolism and arises from the interpenetration of the
image or the metamorphosis of the image in a concentrated hermetic structure, which banishes all possibility
of thought while offering many possible, but not contra-
dictory interpretations of a poem. Johansen admirably
illustrates this matter by showing the possible interpretations of A la nue accablante tu, Tout Orgueil fume-
t-il du soir, and concludes his study with a motif
exegesis of Un Coup de dés in terms of the motif of
the sky and the sea.

The purpose of this dissertation is to
investigate the influence of Mallarmé as a Motif
Symbolist on the minor poets of Symbolism. Concentrating on those poets who were most apt to be somewhat influenced by Mallarmé because of their frequent
contact with him at his Tuesday meetings, we have

---

[21]Ibid., p. 84.

nevertheless decided to be more extensive, and to
consider a larger group of poets, all of whom could
have been affected by his work. Mallarmé's influence
should be expected, but aside from a few minor references in histories of Symbolism, no effort has
been made to evaluate the poetic production of the
minor poets from the starting point of the motif.
We have concerned ourselves with the poetry written
between the years 1885-1900. This investigation will
be an historical study with emphasis mainly on motif
style characteristics of poems within the time limits
indicated. Since our purpose is to study the image
in the light of the Mallarméan motif, problems of
language and versification will not be considered.

     Our main consideration on the following
pages will be the analysis of Motif Symbol poems in
the minor writers. These poems will be then compared
in relationship to each other, to the motifs of Mallarmé,
and classified according to type and degree. As the
poetry to be examined will not, in most instances, be
of the strict motif category, we will then comment on
any effort in the direction of Mallarmé. Starting with
any evidence of Mallarméan vocabulary, syntax, image,
we will proceed from the single instance of the image,
to the strophe, to the entire poem. We shall try to
distinguish mixed works, those with a stylistic
mélange, for example, partly-symbolic, partly-discur-
sive poems, and also those works which show combinations of influence as Mallarmé with Verlaine, Baudelaire, Motif-Impressionistic, and others. Finally
we shall make a synthesis in which an attempt will be
made to establish reasons why some poets and poems were
influenced by Mallarmé, and why others were not.

     The following poets have been selected for
examination: Stuart Merrill, Ephraim Mikhaël, Henri
de Régnier, Georges Rodenbach, Jean Moréas, René Ghil,
Gustave Kahn, Maurice Maeterlinck, Pierre Louÿs, André
Fontainas, Camille Mauclair, Albert Samain, Max Elskamp,
Francis Vielé-Griffin, Albert Mockel, Pierre Quillard,
Jean Royère, André Gide, Ernest Raynaud, and Raymond

de la Tailhède.[22]

I wish to thank Dr. Helmut Hatzfeld for his patient guidance of this dissertation, Dr. Alessandro Crisafulli and Dr. Tatiana Fotitch for their helpful suggestions, Dr. Daniel Crabb, Miss Georgianna McFadden, and Mr. Peter Morris for their assistance in the preparation of the manuscript, and the staffs of the Library of Congress and the Mullen Library of The Catholic University of America for their cooperation.

---

[22]For our purpose it was sufficient to consider the poems contained in the Oeuvres of these authors without going to ephemeral poems published in the periodicals of their time.

CHAPTER I

REMAINDERS OF DISCURSIVE AND DESCRIPTIVE VERSE

A perusal of Symbolism points out the lacuna which exists between the treatment of the major and the suppression of the minor poets. This does not lend virtue to any contention that such minor poets are non-Symbolists; to the contrary, since they form so considerable a group, the implication calls for a redefinition of Symbolism which we shall essay in our conclusion.

Mallarmé is the Symbolist par excellence, once we admit motif symbolism as the ideal. The logical consequence is first, by way of elimination, the examination of the non-Mallarméan quality resident in the works of these writers. An appraisal of what is not new, not distinctly modern brings into profile some aspects of the image as it wavers between prose and poetry before it becomes a fully symbolic, hence poetic image.

There seems thus to be adequate justification for beginning with a survey, however slight, of the opposite pole of Symbolism, the Ecole Romane, which commences sometime during the year 1891, for the reaction of Jean Moréas and his followers to Symbolism is exemplary of a poetic as far removed from Mallarmé as possible, yet contemporaneous with him.

The purpose of the group as announced in Figaro, September 14, 1891[1], was to reclaim and exercise the Greco-Roman principle of poetry which Moréas insisted was fundamental to French verse. As Raymond points out,

---

[1] quoted by Marcel Raymond, De Baudelaire au Surréalisme (Paris, 1947), pp. 58-59.

Moréas, without making the necessary distinctions between ideas and forms of the Medieval period, the Renaissance, and the seventeenth century, believed French
poetry to be based on Greek and Latin traditions from
the eleventh through the eighteenth centuries.[2] Charles
Maurras as the defender of the group, basing himself
on an ideology which identified the period with the
Greek ideal of poetry as he understood it in the foot-
steps of Chénier, was bound then to attack 19th Century
poetry from Romanticism through Mallarmé. The rich
lyricism of the Romantics was condemned as a tendency
which had corrupted the language, degraded the poetic
style, and broken the traditional verse form.[3] Maurras
insisted on a poetry ordered in each part to conform
to a whole which is governed by the discursive intellect.[4]
Thus the whole movement of poetry from the beginnings
of the century on would have to be disregarded.

     Our whole discussion of this movement would be
quite unnecessary had not members of the Ecole Romane
made themselves a part of Symbolism. Moréas adhered
first to Symbolism and even assumed for himself the
leadership of the group. Thus we have considered it
advisable to give some attention to the Neo-Classicists
because of the possibility of a measure of influence
radiating from Mallarmé even on their determined retreat
to the past. We have studied several of the group, Jean
Moréas, Raymond de la Tailhède, and Ernest Raynaud. In
addition we have noted a penchant for classical antiquity
in Pierre Quillard, Henri de Régnier, especially Pierre
Louÿs, and in the first poems of Jean Royère. Drawing
on the results of our investigation, the following
classifications may be presented: The least Symbolist,
most prose-like and Romanist is Raymond de la Tailhède.
In this he supersedes Moréas who is every bit as
descriptive, but who enjoys a wider vision. Both are
innocent of any Mallarméan touch. Ernest Raynaud,
despite his adherence to the group, is often influenced
by Mallarmé, as we shall show later in this study, and

[2]Ibid.   [3]Ibid.   [4]Ibid.

De Régnier and Louÿs have none of the blatant qualities
of the movement insofar as it distinguishes itself from
Parnassianism. The same can be said of Pierre Quillard
who is mostly Parnassian with some Symbolist leanings,
and with Jean Royère, Parnassian-Romanist tendencies are
too few and too early to have any importance for his
whole work.

The complete work of Raymond de la Tailhède is
permeated by the artificiality of the Ecole Romane. His
poetry is constantly descriptive, verbal; the contents,
odes to the new poets, Moréas, Du Plessys, eulogies on
Athens, dithyrambs to Helen, invocation of the Muse,
and personifications of abstracts, because of their
strict and narrow form, the high-sounding and confined
vocabulary, the pompous glorification of a bygone culture,
the incessant authoritative allusions to mythological
beings, give the impression of great bombast. The prose
nature of his work is everywhere apparent. The following
example shows De la Tailhède as a descriptive poet who
is virtually barren of image:

O Muses, vous avez fait naître
Mon ami, Moréas, mon maître,
Dans votre éternelle cité;
Vous l'avez nourri de ces (flammes)
Dont, par vos seins, (brûlent) les âmes
Des grands morts qui l'ont précédé! 5

Moréas shares De la Tailhède's affection for
the pseudosymbols of gods and goddesses, and although
he far surpasses De la Tailhède in poetic range and
capability, his poems too are inundated with prose
elements to the detriment of the image. Sometimes a

5Raymond de la Tailhède, Les Poésies de Raymond de la Tailhède (Paris, 1938), p. 35.

lyric strain emerges in his poetry as in "Hélas! Car c'est déjà la saison monotone/L'Automne sur les fleurs et dans mon coeur l'automne."[6], but it is of such a frail timbre because of the plainly discursive elements that it prevents a true analogy between the interior sentiment and the image.

Any effort he attempts in the direction of the rêve comes off poorly because he cannot subordinate his discursiveness. Thus in a poem patterned on the Symbolist voyage poem to a dream country, the use of color, a very effective element with the lyric-Symbolists, is not at all successful, since it is used for a color kaleidoscope but not for symbolic "climates" in the sense of the vowel sonnet of Rimbaud:

. . . .
. . . .
Nous reverrons, au fond des visions latentes
Le paysage vert, le paysage bleu.
Le paysage vert et rose et jaune et mauve
Où murmure l'eau claire en les fouillis des joncs.[7]

Ernest Raynaud is the least romane of the Romanistes. Despite his affiliation with Moréas and De la Tailhède, he is equally influenced by Verlaine, Baudelaire, and in several poems, even by Mallarmé. Aside from his neo-classic work we can detect a penchant for color and odors which is Baudelairian, a sensualistic presentation of love which surpasses Baudelaire (and perhaps goes in the direction of a poetic realism), and an interest in contemporary society (mainly in his portrait poems). In several sonnets there is an obvious imitation of the Mallarméan

---

[6]Jean Moréas, Oeuvres de Jean Moréas, Vol. I (Paris, 1926), p. 64.

[7]Ibid., pp. 28-29.

form. Descriptive elements, however, become progressively more dominant across his work, and by 1905 his work is almost exclusively so.

Moréas, De la Tailhède, and Raynaud form the bridge between Symbolism and the Ecole Romane. The other poets whom we have mentioned utilized classical antiquity in an entirely different manner, either to express a modern lyrical état d'âme which fuses with Symbolism, or in descriptive-lyrical combinations working out of Parnassianism. Pierre Quillard, for example, embodies a poetic which is a lyric development of Parnassian tendencies. Thus he often composed long narrative poems in which he exploited ancient civilizations, the Middle Ages, and other sources of myth. There are many descriptive elements but these are always coupled with a rich lyric quality proving the poet's personal engagement.

Pierre Louÿs perhaps was the most Hellenistic poet and writer of France. As we know, his whole work is oriented to a pre-Christian paganism. His interest in the past, however, has nothing in common with that of the Ecole Romane. Many of his early poems are Parnassian descriptions of Greek legend, but under the influence of Symbolism he recaptures the past in a thoroughly modern form. The same can be stated of Henri de Régnier who properly merges a classical background with a modern sensibility and poetic.

The Ecole Romane was a temporary challenge to modern poetry. Overstressing a reasoned poetry, its products were usually descriptive and prose-like. Because of these elements it is an extension of the Parnassian urge of a previous generation, a dying objective which no longer produces the objective gems of a Leconte de Lisle.

If the Nineteenth Century was concluding with few vestiges of prose-like poetry, the same cannot be said for lyric verse. Lyricism was given new life through the Romantic movement, and Symbolism did not destroy it. Rather, the lyric poet at the end of the century was in a process of acclimating his work to

new demands and was to play an important role in the
new poetic. Symbolism for many of the minor poets is
the utilization of new vocabularies, a richer imagery
and new forms to propagate their lyric urge in a way
befitting the times. Symbolism may be regarded as a
drastic refinement of lyricism, and it is for this
reason that we like Marcel Raymond's classification
of Mallarmé as a supra-lyric poet.[8]

   Traditional lyric expression is found among
many poets of the 1890's. In greater and lesser degrees, the same feelings which produced the laments
of the 1820's and 1830's are still present and can be
found in the poems of Samain, Merrill, Mikhaël, Vielé-
Griffin, De Régnier, Quillard, Mockel, the early Jean
Royère, to mention only some significant examples.
Lyricism here spoken of in terms of content, and discursiveness in form implies the following categories:
exaltation and cultivation of the moi, a reliance on
subjective reactions to life, cult of the past, poems
of rêve and escape to a happier existence, lyrics of
unrequited love and the transitory nature of existence,
and lastly, a note sounded in the terminal hours of
Romanticism, and chanted again at the close of the
century, a quixotic humanitarianism, a very pronounced
alliance of man and nature, a chanting of simple,
realistic peasant and provincial life. Much of the
subject matter just listed has little to do with Symbolism. The Naturists, for example, as a group are
not allied with the Symbolists for they represent a
movement more on the heels of Symbolism than contemporary
with it. We are primarily interested in lyric qualities
as they show themselves among poets commonly regarded as
Symbolists. Thus Albert Samain would be our prime example of a lyric poet who is Symbolist more by fate of
time than inclination, while the lyricism of Max Elskamp
is so modified by his modernity that he introduces an
entirely original concept to it.

_____

[8]Raymond, op. cit., p. 35.

Choosing one category of content, the cult of
the past, we can illustrate with examples the continu-
ation of a subjective poetry primarily discursive among
the Symbolists. Hardly a Symbolist poet examined was
found to be free of longings for another period of time,
either from his own past or from an age he imagined to
be happier and more tranquil. Like the Romantics, the
lyric-Symbolists envisaged the past in terms of a place
in nature, the atmosphere of a season, the ending of
summer and the coming of fall, in nature images which
link the near and the far (distant horizons, winds,
winding rivers). Henri de Régnier has the largest
number of such poems, but they are found in number
among all the Symbolists who evince a predominantly
lyrical tendency.[9]

---

[9] Mais voici que, tout bas, chuchote la chanson
Que chantent, dans la nuit, les plaintives fontaines
Dans le coeur secoué d'un intime frisson
S'éveille le regret des tendresses lointaines.
    Henri de Régnier, Premiers poèmes ("Vers le
passé," Les Lendemains), (Paris, 1898), p. 16.

Je cherche les endroits où ta robe est allée
Où flotte un souvenir de ta jupe envolée,
Où je retrouve encore dans l'or je ne sais quoi
Qui me fait palpiter le coeur, et qui fut Toi.
    Albert Samain, Le Chariot d'or (Paris, 1947),
p. 78.

    See also Francis Vielé-Griffin's poem "Ronde
des cloches du nord," in Oeuvres de Francis Vielé-
Griffin, Vol. I (Paris, 1924), p. 65, and Gustave
Kahn, Premiers poèmes (Paris, 1897), p. 61.

We have chosen these lyrical poems on the
past because they seem to us to be the most typical
echo of pseudo-Symbolism. Allied emotions such as
melancholy and _ennui_ are likewise to be found in
quantity, especially in the works of Samain and Mikhaël,
and the expression of the poetic vocation – _poeta_
vates – as conceived by Hugo, is universal.

Nature poetry is another major category of
Symbolist lyricism and is best illustrated in the many
nature poems of Vielé-Griffin, and in _Clartés_ of Albert
Mockel. The chanting of love as a joyful experience
(the best example here of course remains Emile Verhaeren)
is to be observed in both Gustave Kahn and André Fontainas.
The lyricism of the Symbolists, however, is only in
content exactly the same as that of the Romantics. In
most instances, of course, there remained the discursiveness typical of any ego-centered poetry, and the image
in many cases was still based on a very exterior analogy,
usually from nature. The poetry of Baudelaire, Verlaine,
and Mallarmé effected many changes upon traditional
lyric poetry. We shall conclude this chapter with a
glance at the influence of Baudelaire and Verlaine on
the minor Symbolists. The transformations which come
about through Mallarmé will be the subject of the
following chapters.

Baudelairian patterns are manifest in most
of the minor Symbolist poets. Poems of escape into
an earthly paradise fashioned after "L'Invitation
au voyage" are common and often fused with Verlainian
impressionism. Many poems are filled with oneiric
imagery, lugubrious landscapes, a sense of impending
doom, dissatisfaction with life, _ennui_, and pre-
occupation with death. In general, the first generation Symbolists found in Baudelaire an ideal example
of their own schizophrenic syndrome. Consequently the

unholy fusion of heaven and earth, flesh and spirit, which is so characteristic of Baudelaire, is a dominant sentiment with these poets. It may be the characteristic paradox of the end of the century.[10]

---

[10]Cette nuit, au-dessus des quais silencieux,
Plane un calme lugubre et glacial d'automne.
Nul vent, les becs de gaz en file monotone
Luisent au fond de leur halo, comme des yeux.

. . . .

Comme un flux de métal épais, le fleuve noir
Fait sous le ciel sans lune un clapotis de vagues.
Et maintenant, empli de somnolences vagues,
Je sombre dans un grand et morne nonchaloir.

Ephraim Mikhaël, "Effet de soir," in Ad. Van Bever and Paul Léautaud, Poètes d'aujourd'hui, Vol. II, (Paris, 1927), pp. 24-25.

Mais l'ombre en flocons noirs a neigé sur nos âmes,
L'ombre que nul soleil ne fondra de ses flammes.
Et déjà le dragon, loin des havres heureux,
Mord les antiques flots glacés et ténébreux.

Pierre Quillard, La Lyre héroïque et dolente ("Mare Tenebrarum"), (Paris, 1897), p. 62.

Mourir et remourir! O volupté suprême!
Vaguer de mort en vie au reflux des remous,
Et dans le crépuscule ainsi qu'un noyé blême
S'affaler sur la grève au fond des sables mous!

Stuart Merrill, Poèmes 1887-1897 (Les Gammes), (Paris, 1897), p. 35. See also Louis Le Cardonnel, Poèmes (Paris, 1904), p. 20, and Albert Samain, Chariot, p. 109.

The _angoisse_ of the Romantics is so developed by these
latter day lyric poets, the abyss between the real and
the ideal is pushed to such extremes, the spiritual
aridity of the end of the century is so intense, that
its lyric poetry has no choice but to face the _gouffre_
and produce a lyric poetry of real metaphysical import.
What is more important, however, is the imprint of
Baudelaire on poetic construction, the deepening of
the analogy brought about through _correspondance_ and
synesthesia. Excepting such a rigid Neo-Classicist
as Raymond de la Tailhède, synesthesia is such a
common practice among the Symbolists that it is difficult to realize that this device was a rarity before
Baudelaire. The importance of this widespread development cannot be stressed enough, for it indicates a new
psychological perception of reality, a shift in the
vision for what Johansen calls the pre-poetic tonality,
a shift away from the realistic vision of the universe
to a new ordering of the elements in the mind, which
in turn can engender a new mode of expression. Liberating
the image from rational demands, priority to the image
over description, a greater unity between individual
images, Baudelaire made much of this possible and the
theme Symbolism of Baudelaire which we referred to in
our introduction is a poetic device quite widely
dispersed among the minor Symbolist poets.

Finally, the vogue for impressionistic poetry
as written by Verlaine is another major aspect of
Symbolist lyricism. After Verlaine, poets turned to
a descriptive poetry (mostly of 18th Century Watteau
pastoral scenes), and to the exploitation of their own
feelings with a poetry characterized by primacy of
atmosphere, desire for the vague and the imprecise,
and the predominance of musical effect. Albert
Samain is the disciple _par_ _excellence_ of Verlaine,
but many of the poets investigated showed an imitation
of his work.[11] Verlaine's poetry is above all musical

---

[11]In a poem entitled "Dilection," Samain expresses what is almost an _art_ _poétique_ of his work. It

and illustrates another step in the development of
modern lyricism. Although we would not consider him a
Symbolist in the sense in which the term is applied to
Mallarmé, the penchant for mystery, atmosphere, night
over day, plus his rich sound patterns, is an important
step in moving the lyric toward a hermetic form.

---

is the closest imitation of Verlaine's "Art poétique"
among the Symbolists:

> J'adore l'indécis, les sons, les couleurs frêles,
> Tout ce qui tremble, ondule, et frissonne, et chatoie,
> Les cheveux et les yeux, l'eau, les feuilles, la soie,
> Et la spiritualité des formes grêles;
> Albert Samain, Au Jardin de l'Infante (Paris,
> 1947), p. 45.

> Alternant d'une voix frêle
> Cette musique indécise
> Que berçait d'un souffle l'aile
> Exquise de quelque brise.
> Camille Mauclair, Sonatines d'automnes (Paris,
> 1895), p. 25.

> Dans le golfe aux jardins ombreux
> Des couples blonds d'amants heureux
> Ont fleuri les mats langoureux
>   De ta galère
> Et caresse du doux été
> Notre beau navire enchanté
> Vers les pays de volupté
>   Fend l'onde claire !
> Ephraim Mikhaël, Oeuvres de Mikhaël (Paris,
> Lemerre, n.d.), p. 101. See also Maurice Maeterlinck,
> Serres chaudes (Brussels, 1900), p. 13, and Francis
> Vielé-Griffin, Oeuvres, II, p. 24.

12

We have purposely ignored in this chapter such
traditional forms as allegory, personification, repetition, and refrain, for they are devices which can be
utilized also by pure Symbolism in its search for a
unity. Hence they will be considered in the next
chapter. What we have tried to insist on in this
chapter are those aspects of poetry which, properly
speaking, cannot be called Symbolist in the sense of
the poems of Mallarmé, but yet were poetic forms
contemporaneous with him. These, we summarize, were
the rigid intellectual poetry of the Ecole Romane,
the traditional lyric pattern of the Romantics, ending
up in Naturism, and the development of lyricism in the
imitations of Baudelaire and Verlaine. Despite the
advances made by the latter poets, their work cannot
be considered symbolic if we deduce the law from the
poetic type of Mallarmé. Now that we have examined
some traditional forms, pseudo-symbolic and pre-symbolic,
let us look at the poetic image, at the center, as it
works toward a symbolic synthesis, prototypically present in the works of Mallarmé.

CHAPTER II

PROGRESS IN THE STRUGGLE FOR A UNIFIED SYMBOLISM

The famous lines of Paul Verlaine, "Il pleure
dans mon coeur," would be a fitting preface to this
dissertation because they seem to hold the germ of the
modern poem. Across the last century, from the whimper-
ing of the Romantics, the cry of despair of Baudelaire,
the lament of Verlaine, to the "L'Azur, l'Azur, l'Azur,
l'Azur !" of Mallarmé, the poet has become increasingly
aware of his unsettled and disturbed condition. A
universal ennui is discernible in nearly all of the
poets of the end of the century who in most cases find
this life unbearable, and in some, an eternity unbelievable.
Out of this anguish emerges an effort to express
these inexpressible longings, the complexities of life,
the mysteries of nature. The poet will no longer be
satisfied with a poetry which can say no more than prose,
which can only state that he is in love, or that autumn
is a melancholy season. Through analogies he will look
for relationships, sometimes consciously, sometimes not
so, for rapports, unities between himself and the world
about him. He will create a poetry which can somewhat
express the ambiguous and complex creature he is. In a
word, the new poetry will seek to evoke why "mon coeur
a tant de peine" or "de joie." To bring forward the
hidden, the mysterious in man, the poet will create by
the secret order of his intuition, by the reason of the
heart about which the reason knows not at all. This must
be taken as a goal even there where the "intuition" is
constructed. And to do this, a new order will be imposed,
a poetry will be written with images, sounds, and rhythms
assuming an unprecedented importance, a poetry from which
the intellectual order demanded by the Parnassians and
Romanistes will be excluded.

14

The _ennui_ poems, the voyage and dream poems
are all indicative of the new verse. They are manifestations of internal dissatisfaction, vague murmurings,
of possible venturings, possible discoveries and creations.
A grasping for the unknown is seen in poems
made after the manner of the Verlaine poems we have just
mentioned. This note runs through the work of Raynaud,
Kahn, and Rodenbach.[1] First then in the steps toward a
symbolic unity is the awareness of the possibility of
an expression of the inexplicable. The perception of
an interior life gave rise to such poems as those just
mentioned. Most such poems, however, are primarily
descriptive, the _je ne sais quoi_ discursively proclaimed.
This leads to a primary distinction to be made in any
consideration of the Symbolists. The poet who is unable
to arrive at a poetic unity through an autonomous thought-
free imagery, but who yet has a yearning to express the

---

[1] Je ne sais ce qui m'oppresse
Mon rire mouillé de pleurs
Manifeste une allegresse
Voisine de la douleur.
Ernest Raynaud, _La Couronne des jours_ (Paris,
1905), p. 120.

As-tu cherché le pourquoi des émois sans cause
C'est dès longtemps
Tout est bien fini que nous cause
Les remembrances des printemps.
Gustave Kahn, _Premiers poèmes_, p. 49.

"Toute une vie en nous, non visible, circule..."
Georges Rodenbach, _Oeuvres de Georges
Rodenbach_, Vol. II (_Les Vies encloses_, 1896) (Paris,
1923), p. 133.

"Nous ne savons de notre âme que la surface..."
Ibid., p. 136.

rumblings in his soul, will probably create a poem on the order of the ones we have quoted. Thus it is that on one level a circumlocution of the symbol through actual prose substitutions for the image will take place, or any number of devices will be used in the imagery to substitute for a symbolization, and on another level, within the frame of a hermetic structure, mannerism will replace symbolization.[2]

Albert Samin, to a degree that it is one of his characteristic methods of creating analogy, and Georges Rodenbach, to a lesser degree, search for a means to go beyond the usual term of comparison. Thus they often substitute terms such as "Il semble" and "On dirait."[3] This is primarily an attempt to achieve a greater unity between the images by fundamentally discursive terms, well known since Victor Hugo. Many of the poets showed examples of such technique, but these were always too few to have any significance. The fact that it is so dominant with Samain means that his effort toward Symbolism was, in a great many instances, unable to rise beyond an intensifying of the traditional term of comparison, comme, with sembler and dire substitutions. He remains primarily discursive with little unity or development of image.

---

[2] Johansen makes this distinction very clear when he compares poems of Mallarmé and Maeterlinck. Johansen, op. cit., p. 85.

[3] Le ciel comme un lac d'or pâle s'évanouit,
   On dirait que la plaine, au loin déserte, pense;
      Samain, Chariot, p. 84.

Sur la Ville brûlante, un instant apaisée,
On dirait qu'une main de femme s'est posée;
   Ibid., p. 19.

Several examples of image dispersion are indicative of the essay toward symbolic unity made by the minor poets. An early sonnet of André Fontainas, from which we quote the first tercet[4], is a fine example of this device. The poet is expressing the impression he receives of a woman's voice. This is accomplished by the accumulation of images which the poet believes to be analogous to the voice. When the image is powerful enough and is able to transcend thought, a theme symbolism in which the poetic tonality is effected by the interaction of the image is produced. Such is not the case with this poem of Fontainas. The images are too many and too dispersed to bring about even a theme unity. The poem dates from Fontainas's first collection, and its effusion should be considered a consequence of its lyricism. If we would consider it for its evocation, we would have to say that the poet, unable to express what he means, accumulates image upon image in the hope that his feeling can be communicated. What is positively significant is the placing of emphasis on the image and not on any intellectualized abstraction.

Maeterlinck is not only discursive as Johansen has shown, but retains as a poetic principle the disunity of image as a means of arriving at a unity of expression. The intellectual equation is quite obvious in a number of poems, and when it is not, the image appears ungoverned, personally associative, and often

---

[4]Sa voix, c'est la douceur des songes innocents,
C'est un souffle d'iris, de cinname et d'encens,
C'est un enivrement d'harmonie et d'optique,

André Fontainas, Le Sang des fleurs (Bruxelles, 1889), p. 27.

obscure. Intellectualization coupled with oneiric
tendencies thus produce in Maeterlinck such images as
"L'ennui d'un matelot dans le désert...," and "Un
navire à pleines voiles sur un canal...."[5] Both images
are from a poem expressing the lack of harmony in existence. Kahn makes the same type of accumulation with
the image stemming from thought, although his imagery
seems to be analogically sound in comparison to the
startling contrasts of Maeterlinck.[6]

---

[5]Maeterlinck, op. cit., pp. 9-10.

[6]Solitude d'éponge endormie
Et silence des momies
Et paix vaste des accalmies-
Aux ongles déchireurs de mes flancs introuvables.
    Kahn, Premiers poèmes, p. 94.

Kahn has many variations of this basic technique.
In "La Mer dans la nuit" he uses a repetition, "Voix,"
which stands for the ocean with a series of comparisons
which enjoy a unity of fright and terror:

Voix monocorde et de terreur
Voix de spectres traînant des fers
Voix d'orpheline énorme de douleurs
                    Voix de menace
Voix d'ogre qui se désespère
De la pâture rare et d'entraves à sa chasse
Voix de lourd péril instant
Cris de bourreaux, voix du néant.
    Gustave Kahn, La Pluie et le beau temps
(Paris, 1896), p. 7.

Repetition and Refrain

Repetition of word, line, and strophe, the exploitation of rhythms already established in peasant rounds and church prayers, experimentation with sound values of vowels and consonants, and alliterations are salient characteristics of Symbolist poetry.

Poetry as music is the most discernible feature of the poetry of Verlaine, and as we have indicated, imitations were far from rare. Verhaeren's evocations of his native Flanders and modern industrialization are more often than not achieved through an effective employment of sound, and the same may be said for the Flemish lyric poet Max Elskamp. René Ghil, first adopting a vowel system after the sonnet of Rimbaud, developed a complicated theory on poetic instrumentation to which he remained faithful against all evidence, and of which his work is the unique witness.

The theories on poetry as music are of interest to us because they are indicative of the desire for unity. For this reason, a slight consideration and evaluation of some poems where sound and rhythm achieve more importance than the image is necessary. Overdeveloped in some poets, music was nevertheless highly esteemed by all of them, and when combined judiciously with other elements had a proper and fitting place in Symbolist poetry. Mallarmé's work is evidence of a subtle musicality and his Les mots anglais is evidence that the master symbolist saw a primary rapport between music (the subjectivity of sound) and poésie pure.

"L'Ile heureuse" of Mikhaël[7] is an example of the unity achieved by a poem which is in the manner of Verlaine. In this poem there is no action; rather the voyage to a land of rêve is seen through the sound relationships and the impressionistic syntax which produces an état d'âme. The images invade the reader like a series of perfumes of slightly different odors to produce a feeling of volupté and rêve. In the first

---

[7]See note 11, Chapter I, page 11.

three lines the last words, ombreux, heureux, and
langoureux are related in evocation and in sound pattern.
That these words are interacting in a secondary unity
which works out of the primary sound unit is evident
in the fact that the adjectives do not necessarily have
to apply to their own noun: langoureux, for example,
without upsetting the original proposition, may apply
to jardins, indicating a mellow summer landscape touched
by a lazy breeze, or to amants, indicating a corresponding
psychology in the personages. This is possible because
the words are so closely related in meaning and sound
that they cannot maintain any type of successful independence. The syntax should also be noted. The position of ont fleuri indicates that it refers to les
mats langoureux, but it may also apply to d'amants
heureux. The de ta galère increases the non-discursive
effect already activated by the sounds, for after everything else in the plural follows this singular possessive
adjective referring to a non-present (in the poem) subject. This adds mystery and tone aside from its conven-
ience over votre. Stuart Merrill has many examples of
this method, as for example, the refrain in his "Fête
au parc."[8] The refrain frames a series of 18th. century
tableaux, and summarizes the whole poem. Without verb,
we are forced to concentrate on non-discursive elements,
sound, color, nouns which evocate music and clothing in
a general manner. The whole refrain tends toward a non-
discursive lyric, even ambiguous statement.

---

[8] O le frisson des falbalas,
Le bruissement des brocatelles,
La lassitude des lilas,
La vanité des bagatelles.
    Merrill, Poèmes, p. 11.

Musical effect is a ruling force in the poetry of Merrill. He was much impressed by both the content and manner of expression of Verlaine, and he was an intimate associate of René Ghil. He approaches Verlaine in his Petits Poèmes d'automne (1895) which is similar to Romances sans paroles, and his first collection, Les Gammes (1887), is in subject matter very similar to Fêtes galantes. A comparison of poems, however, illustrates that Merrill emphasizes sound with a vigor almost unknown to Verlaine. Merrill is especially to be noticed for his alliterations. Coupled with vowel frequency, they produce a startling unity in sound. "La Flûte"9 from Les Gammes is an example of Merrill's adaptation of "L'Après-Midi d'un faune" to a sound medium. This poem, dedicated to Mallarmé, is an evocation of the rites of spring. Its unity proceeds from two sources, the central image of Pan and his flute, and the support given to the image by the alliterations. Merrill, interested in achieving the same sentiment as Mallarmé, "Ces nymphes, je les veux perpétuer," enhances and centralizes the flute by the alliterations, patterns of s,f,v, and p, which suggest the sounds of the flute, the whispers, rustlings, and whistles which carry the sound everywhere. Verlaine used sound to set a tone, to give an atmospheric unity. This poem by Merrill not only sets a tone, but directs the poem, the sounds indicating what is being evoked. The poem approaches motif symbolism in the singleness of its expression, one image, Pan and his flute, to express the renewal of life substantiated by a sound unity. The poem, of course, is always under the discursive direction of the poet.

9La voix du divin Pan s'avive de folie,
Et son souffle qui siffle en la flûte polie
Eveille les désirs du renouveau viril...
    Ibid., p. 7.

Max Elskamp makes extensive use of sound patterns, of a rougher kind than Verlaine, however, rather in the manner of Verhaeren, and often the image is subordinated to the point of obliteration. The most striking example of this process is a poem from Dominical[10] where an impressionism of sound, brought about through sound similarities and alliterations, forms the whole evocation of an aspect of Flemish life from the childhood of the poet.

Johansen has shown how refrains moulded into a popular rhythm pattern or poems based on an already existing rhythm, in prayers for example, can result in poetic unification.[11] Our study of the minor Symbolist poets only confirms his statements. These poets were attracted to repetition and refrain techniques because the pure rythmical qualities inherent in such forms produce a trance-like state which relegates thought to the background. Symbolism and lyricism meet in the refrain when the poet either borrows existing forms or creates new ones in the same manner.

No poet makes as extensive use of common secular and religious refrains as Max Elskamp who draws on his Flemish background, the prayers of the church, the games of childhood, the peasant atmosphere, particularly that of the fisherman, to produce an original lyricism. Remembrances of childhood, for example, are

---

[10]Et s'ébrouant
Rouets rouants
Les rouets, au matin des vieilles,
Leur font s'éjouir les oreilles
D'un bruit rouant
Et s'ébrouant.
    Max Elskamp, *La Louange de la vie*
(*Dominical*), (Paris, 1898), p. 22.

[11]Johansen, *op. cit.*, p. 211.

caught up in the children's song "Frère Jacques." First
Elskamp uses the song to lyrically exploit the image
(which is always fading away under the impact of the
incessant rhythm of the refrain) of childhood, greedy
little children on a Sunday morning after Mass. The
same rhythm is used to evocate the past, his sleeping
villages. Here the refrain works in several directions,
"dormez-vous" meaning the past and also expressing the
tranquillity of Flemish village life.12 Elskamp also
makes use of the salutation to Mary, the "Hail Mary."
This rhythm, without doubt embedded in the very soul
of the Flemish poet, is successfully developed in
several different ways. In the example there is a
play on words. Elskamp substitutes pêcheur for pécheur

12Ils sont venus, ils sont venus,
Naïvement nus et goulus
De raisins de verre et de cierges
Sur les bras longs des Saintes Vierges,
Les dimanches; sonnez matines,
Frère Jacques, en mes doctrines.
    Elskamp, Louange, p. 17.

Et la ville de mes mille âmes,
Dormez-vous, dormez-vous;
Il fait dimanche, mes femmes,
Et ma ville, dormez-vous?
    Ibid., p. 19.

and turns the rhythm to a lyric expression of the life
of the fishermen.[13]

As we have remarked, the technique of repetition and refrain is a major Symbolist device. The frequency varies from poet to poet, and likewise it is
used in diverse manners. We have observed that sometimes the refrain is so infrequent as to be barely
perceptible; more commonly it is used to frame a strophe
or an entire poem; at times it is used as a means of
recapitulation, and finally the repetitions can appear
so consecutively, and with such minor variations, that
they form a whole.

René Ghil uses the lyric refrain in a very
modern manner, and in some ways precurses the work of
Saint-John Perse. Ghil conceived of his work as a
great symphony, and consequently, each poem while
having an integrity, is designed to be viewed ultimately in the light of a series of poems. In Part I
of Voeu de Vivre, for example, which is according to
the editors "...une analyse, une synthèse continue du
Monde des activités modernes..."[14], the Eiffel Tower,
personified, acts as a unifying device to which all
images are not connected, but to which the poet returns
as a lyric refrain, a starting point, a new point of
departure for more images of industrial Paris.

Repetitions and refrains are ordinarily found
in well-ordered and planned relationships. The most
common occurence is the rondeau technique, when the

---

[13]Et je m'en reviens de mer,
    Pauvre pêcheur,
Maintenant et à l'heure
    De ce dimanche
    Ainsi soit-il.
      Ibid., p. 83.

[14]René Ghil, Oeuvres complètes, Vol. I (Paris,
1938), p. 117.

opening and closing lines of a strophe are the same.[15]
The effect intended in such instances is lyrical, and
the repetition sets a rhythmical tone rather than inter-
vening directly in the other images. This is particularly true with Elskamp where the lyricism has the
effect of being almost pure song.

Camille Mauclair is the most clever practitioner
of repetition among the Symbolist poets. He creates
many variations of repetition, and it is his ordering
of them which makes this device so unusually effective
in his poetry. He has been so thoroughly discussed
by Johansen, however, that any further discussion on
our part would be superfluous.[16]

Repetition as a determining factor is also
exhibited in the poems of Vielé-Griffin and De Régnier.
This fact has been somewhat overlooked by Johansen in
his classification of the poems of Vielé-Griffin as
"allusion" poems, that is, nature poems which are
neither objective enough to approach realism nor subjectively transformed enough to be called symbols.

---

[15]Lors, vive la rose
Des vents, et vois là, passager
La terre où parlent mensongers
Les loins pays dont d'autres causent;
Lors, vive la rose.
Elskamp, Louange, op. cit., p. 86.

Un soir l'Orgue d'église aux spasmes des Violons
Montait loin sa douleur sourde en les râles longs:
Voix de genèse, Amour et Trépas, ô pleurs longs!
Un soir l'Orgue montait dans l'horreur des Violons...
René Ghil, Oeuvres, op. cit., Vol. III
(Légendes d'âmes et de sangs, "Dies Irae"), p. 10.

[16]Johansen, op. cit., p. 176.

Rather, they are poems in which thought is banished,
the image is primary (as in true symbol poems), but the
evocation is purely emotional. No thought is possible.[17]
Johansen illustrates the "Allusion" technique with two
poems from Vielé-Griffin, "Un Oiseau chantait" and "Les
doux soirs sont flétris." While agreeing with Johansen
on the existence of the quasi-symbolic "Allusion" poem,
we feel that in the poems which he has cited, particularly in "Un Oiseau chantait," that it is not so much
the individual nature image which effects the tonality,
but rather the constant repetition and variation of a
single refrain which haunts the whole structure.[18] In
such a light, the same technique of repetition which
effects the tonality of the legend poems of Mauclair
would be the source of the elevation of the nature lyric
from an *état d'âme* type poem to an "Allusion." Thus the
clouding of the whole atmosphere by the refrain would be
the means by which repetition is used by the Symbolist
poets to arrive at a synthesis, regardless of the subject
matter. The refrain acts in exactly the same manner in
a love lyric of Vielé-Griffin[19], and it is the density

---

[17]*Ibid.*, pp. 170-171.

[18]The refrain, "Derrière chez mon pere, un
oiseau chantait," with its variations, is repeated eight
times in the poem.

[19]Celle qui passe m'a souri,
  —L'Azur est plus pale et l'air est rose—
  Celle qui passe, sans une pause,
  Vaguement tendre comme une chose;
  Comme un ruisseau, comme un pré fleuri:
  Celle qui passe m'a souri-
    Vielé-Griffin, *Oeuvres*, *op. cit.*, Vol. I,
p. 109.

of the repetition in the selection we have chosen from
De Régnier which creates the tonality.[20]

Stuart Merrill provides us with an example of
sustentation of the image in his "Paradis bleu."[21] The
repetitions, built as a rondeau, are intricate, and
the image, by its exaltation and exclamation has few
discursive elements. Each strophe of this poem is
exactly like a ronde, a still life, a theme or aspect
of the fullness of young love. In eight line strophes,
only three lines, action lines, are not repeated, and
around these lines is constructed an incantation, a
trance-like process by which Merrill hopes to achieve
the evocation, in the best Old French rondeau tradition.
Thus in the first strophe which we have quoted, the
significance of the lovers kissing the loved ones is
conveyed in the lyric refrain. Connectives are omitted
and the image consequently has a certain degree of

---

[20] O mon âme, le soir est triste sur hier,
O mon âme, le soir est triste sur demain,
O mon âme, le soir est triste sur toi-même!
    Henri de Régnier, Poèmes 1887-1892 (Tel
qu'en songe, 1892), (Paris, 1895), p. 123.

[21] Dans l'azur des apothéoses
Gloires aux amants fervents et doux!
Ils vont en baissant leurs fronts roses
Dans l'azur des apothéoses
La rougeur des lèvres écloses
Eclate sous leurs cheveux roux.
Dans l'azur des apothéoses
Gloire aux amants fervents et doux!
    Merrill, Poèmes (Gammes), p. 19.

autonomy.

To conclude, we may state that the repetition
technique is one of the distinguishing marks of the
minor Symbolist poets. It is characteristic of Mallarmé
in his early poems when he is still influenced by Baudelaire, but significantly enough this form is abandoned
in his mature work. Repetition is a weak unifying device because emphasis is given mainly to an exterior
unity. When there is a degree of interior unity, as
with the "allusion" poems, no idea can be ascertained
because of the emotional nature of the works; the
symbolization is a matter of tone or mood, and not of
image. The fact that refrain was so widely used is
proof that the minor Symbolists were aiming at a poetic
synthesis in the musical sense, but were unable to
reach beyond a form early abandoned by Mallarmé.

Camille Mauclair represents the maximum development here, and in so far as he is a Symbolist, refrain
techniques are his closest approximations of Mallarmé.

Personification and Allegory

Personification and allegory are also usual
techniques of the minor Symbolists, for like repetition
and refrain, they produce a unified structure. Unlike
repetition, the allegory can truly interiorize, and
with several poets actually undergoes a transformation
into the Mallarméan motif symbol poem.

Personification is found in all of the poets;
with some it is employed in a traditional manner; others
use it as much as possible to imitate Mallarmé.

Albert Samain is very fond of personification,
and it is a mainstay of his lyric expression. In most
instances it is a personification of abstracts: silence,

solitude, sadness, pity, peace, truth, love, _ennui_, and
pride. Some samples are: "Le Silence entre nous
marche...," and "C'est la Pitié qui pose ainsi son
doigt sur nous,...."[22] De Régnier has the same tendency
toward personification. There is in fact, a discernible
increase in its use across his work. Somewhat present
in the last group of poems in Premiers poèmes, very evident in Poèmes 1887-1892, especially in the collection
Tel qu'en songe, personification and allegory are the
only "symbolic" elements left amid a forest of description
in Les Jeux rustiques et divins. Because De Régnier's
personifications are more often than not prolonged in
allegory, in contrast to Samain where the personifications are short and almost devoid of any image development, they have greater lyric power, and a depth which
approximates Symbolism is possible. Often the images
are latent with supporting possibilities. In a personification of sadness, "La Tristesse qui passe/Chante
en sa flûte d'or derrière mes cyprès,..."[23], the
realistic point of departure was probably the whistling
of the wind in the trees, powerful enough in itself to
evocate melancholy. The qualification of the sound as
coming from a golden flute, behind the cypress trees,
adds further implications which intensify the evocation.
The flute image echoes an analogy which has been tested
by its repeated use in French letters, the golden trumpet
of Roland announcing defeat at Ronceveaux, and the
plaintive lyric of De Vigny on the same subject, while
in a few years Apollinaire was to employ the same image
to express his melancholy at the loss of his Lou. The
Cypress is a sad tree, the decor for cemeteries. Such
echoes make this personification rich with possibilities.

---

[22]Samain, Jardin, p. 27 and p. 31.

[23]De Régnier, Poèmes 1887-1892, p. 148.

Lyric personification without any echo whatsoever persists in the poetry of Vielé-Griffin and
Albert Mockel. Mockel's personifications of nature are
in a romantic tradition. They are discursive, clear,
traditional (but unusual for French lyricism until the
Naturists), and sentimental.[24] Vielé-Griffin personifies nature without being sentimental. In "Aurore,"[25]
dawn is personified as a young girl making her debut
into the world. By concentrating on an analogy between
the girl and dawn (their common attributes), plus a
very sure use of rhythm and sound, Vielé-Griffin has
created a personification in which the reader can believe for the length of the poem. The poet has succeeded
in making a problem, or rather a mystery out of daybreak,
for the possibility exists in the poem that day will not
arrive.

---

[24] Mets ta main dans la mienne, ô ma belle attentive.
Mai juvénile sourit dans les fleurs.
Rien n'est plus doux, rien n'est plus grave que
                            cette heure,
Et je veux m'incliner sur les divines rives
Où glissent tes regards comme une onde ingénue.
    Albert Mockel, Clartés (Paris, 1902), p. 109.

[25] Claire et pâle, l'aube éclose
Aux plis des collines luit et pose
Son frêle baiser de chose en chose
—Clair et pâle, de chose en chose—
L'Aube est pâle comme une qui n'ose;
Alors on a dit: le jour a peur
Qu'il envoie une telle avant-courrière;
Il hésite et s'attarde en arrière;
Car on ne sait ni qui vit ni qui meurt;
Le jour a peur...
    Vielé-Griffin, Oeuvres, I, op. cit., p. 113.

Georges Rodenbach was perhaps the most conscious imitator of Mallarmé among the minor Symbolists. Here Rodenbach and Mockel coincide for they both attempt the Mallarméan poem through personification. It is Rodenbach who as an avid seeker of analogies actually introduced what can be considered modern personifications. What is significant with Rodenbach is the personification of things rather than the traditional figuration of abstracts. A poem entitled "La Vie des chambres" provides the key to his whole system. Here is the first strophe:

Les chambres, qu'on croirait d'inanimés décors,
—Apparat de silence aux étoffes inertes—
Ont cependant une âme, une vie aussi certes,
Une voix close aux influences du dehors
Qui répand leur pensée en halos de sourdines...[26]

The life which Rodenbach saw in objects is surprisingly Mallarméan for in many instances he chose objects which express incompletion with the same meaning as Mallarmé of "Une dentelle s'abolit" or "Surgi de la croupe et du bond." Thus he personifies an unplayed piano, a water fountain reaching for the sky, or a pond of water desiring to keep a reflection:[27]

---

[26] Rodenbach, Oeuvres, op. cit., Vol. I (Le Regne du silence), p. 179.

[27] Dans l'angle obscur de la chambre, le piano
Songe, attendant des mains pâles de fiancée
De qui les doigts sont sans reproche et sans anneau,
Des mains douces par qui sa douleur soit pansée
Et qui rompent un peu son abandon de veuf,
Car il refrémirait sous des mains élargies
Puisqu'en lui dort encor l'espoir d'un bonheur neuf,
Après tant de silence, après tant d'élégies.
Ibid., p. 184.

Albert Mockel makes similar personifications
in Clartés where he personifies a flower glass which
never takes of any beauty but its own, a wine cup
which partakes of life without ever becoming a part
of it, or a water pond similar to that of Rodenbach.[28]

Les jets d'eau, tout le jour, disent des élégies;
C'est la forme la moins consolable de l'Eau,
Car elle porte haut dans l'air ses nostalgies,
Montant et retombant sous son propre fardeau...
Tristesse des jets d'eau qui sont de l'eau brandie;
Mais nul n'entend leur mal et rien n'y rémédie,
Jets d'eau toujours en peine, impatients du ciel!
Las! l'azur défia leur sveltesse de lance,
Symbole édifiant d'une âme qui s'élance
Et pulvérise au vent son sanglot éternel.
Car l'essor des jets d'eau défaille en cascatelles
Et leur coeur est aussi comme d'un éxilé,
Coeur caché qu'on entend pleurer dans des dentelles.
Or, le moindre mirage est tout annihilé
Dans les vasques en fièvre à la moire élargie.
Pour vouloir trop de ciel, elles perdent le leur!
    Ibid., p. 208. This poem is almost a reworking
of "Le vierge, le vivace et le bel aujourd'hui."

[28]The flower glass prefers its pure beauty to any
color which is cheap by comparison:

Toi, par dédain, du royaume éxilée
où l'arc d'Iris touche les cieux,
tu ériges d'un songe incolore ta tige
aux silencieuses clartés.

O splendeur de ta nudité
Telle jaillie, éblouissante
En sa translucide Beauté!

Mille images sur toi sont passées
que tes yeux reclos n'ont pas vues,...

    Mockel, Clartés, pp. 23-24. See also
pp. 30-35, and 41.

These poems are Mallarméan in content but not in form.
They are primarily discursive, and seem more like the
pre-poetic tonality of Mallarmé rather than the completely transformed image. Beyond the point of grasping an analogy fit to evocate incompletion there are
no similarities. Rodenbach and Mockel personify because they are incapable of bannishing thought. Rodenbach gives the impression that the problem of incompletion interests him more as a philosopher than as poet.
A second reason for their use of personification is
revealed in the lyrical coloring of the poems where
an earthbound, lyrical sentimentality infects a fundamental problem of existence. The sentimentality of
Mockel is particularly apparent through his technique
of actually allowing the objects to speak. Nevertheless,
the work of both poets shows the influence of Mallarmé
within a traditional and discursive poetic form.

Allegory continues in its traditional form with
abstracts figured discursively in well-outlined images.[29]
Romanticism, however, imbued the traditional form with
so many lyric qualities that they become the characteristic mark of this genre in the nineteenth century.

----

[29]L'an qui s'éveille ouvre les portes de l'Année!
En son manteau tissé de songes et de jours
Il voit, fils déjà las de l'antique Toujours,
Que le jardin du Temps fleurit sous l'aube née.

Chacun y va cueillir sa propre destinée
Sous l'étoile propice ou sous l'astre en décours,
Et moissoner, avec des doigts subtils et lourds
La fleur du népenthès ou de la solanée.

De Régnier, Premiers poèmes, p. 292. See
Kahn, Premiers poèmes, p. 102, and Jean Royère, Exil
doré (Paris, 1898), pp. 23-24.

Lyric development here means supremacy of image over
thought; consequently the more obvious types of alle-
gorization, with every term explained, are less frequent, and explanations if offered at all are usually
reserved to the last strophe.

Vigny, whose didactic comparisons were considered "Symbolic" until Baudelaire, is perhaps the ori-
ginator of lyric allegory. His signs are chosen from
diverse fields, nature, animal life, medieval legend,
Biblical accounts, and allegory from Baudelaire on
exploits with greater intensity the same subjects and
signs. The impact of Baudelaire on allegorical figuration cannot be stressed enough. It is his rich lyric
quality which transforms allegory, complicates it into
something like a symbol. The lyricism of Baudelaire
leads to the swan of Mallarmé. Eigeldinger has stated:

> L'Allégorie est pour le poète des Fleurs du Mal
> comme l'a montré A. Guex "une métaphore continuée,
> un parallélisme entre le concret et l'abstrait,
> une fiction transparente par laquelle le poète
> éveille une Idée, cachée d'abord sous le sens
> apparent." Baudelaire l'a renouvelée, enrichie
> par les thèmes lyriques et plus encore par ces
> qualités d'atmosphère dont il possède le secret.
> Ses allégories se développent d'une manière lo-
> gique et cohérente....Le goût de la fiction s'est
> accentué chez Baudelaire avec les années et si
> l'on étudie ses allégories, on ne tarde pas à
> remarquer qu'elles deviennent à la fois plus
> nombreuses et plus complexes, qu'elles tendent
> à se dépouiller de leur contenu matériel, qu'elles
> s'acheminent vers le symbole jusqu'à se confondre
> avec lui.[30]

---

[30] Marc Eigeldinger, L'Evolution dynamique
de l'image (Neuchâtel, 1943), pp. 138-139. Eigeldinger
quotes A. Guex, Aspects de l'art baudelairien, p. 86.

Poetic self-awareness which is so typical of
the Romantics reaches an apex of introspection with
the Symbolists, and this causes an increase in the
number of allegories on poetic vocation, the exile of
the poet, poetic suffering, and the cult of the ideal.
The Middle Ages discovered anew with its wealth of
legendary material by the research of German philologists
in the last years of the century, the cult of Wagner
in the mid-80's, the revival of a Watteau-like 18th
century through the poetry of Verlaine, and the creation
of allegorical lands of rêve provided the raw material
for allegorical expression of the poetic vocation.

Search for the ideal is the source of many
of these poems.[31]The search, usually announced in terms
of a pure conquest, hence the numerous references to
the Medieval period, to Parsifal, and to the search
for the Holy Grail, is nevertheless impeded in its
purity by the very lyricism which composes it. The
longest and best known poem of Vielé-Griffin, "La
Chevauchée d'Yeldis" (1893) is a lyric allegory on the
pursuit of beauty, and is a mixture of the spiritual
and physical ideal as it is expressed in the minor Symbolists. The narrative is of such length that it allows

---

[31]
En vain j'ai parcouru les halliers et les grèves,
Je me suis efforcé
Vers le Nord implacable et le Pole glacé
Aux Thules mornes où meurent les rêves;
Vers les visions impérissables poursuivies
En d'hyperboréennes contrées
Je me suis détourné des routes de la vie.
Les magiciennes rencontrées !
Par elles je crus au mirage de mes rêves
Et je me suis éfforcé
Vers mon illusion par les déserts glacés
Des Thules mornes où meurent les rêves
. . . .
André Fontainas, Choix de Poèmes (Paris,
1950), p. 17.

the poet to almost build up a characterization of Yeldis, but it is never quite so definite. There is never a clear equation between the descriptions and the abstract. Yeldis lives with her father and is loved by five men. Upon the death of her father, she leaves everything behind and rides off into the horizon. The lovers follow in pursuit, but one by one they abandon the chase until only the poet and one other man (active life) are left. Catching up with her, Yeldis surrenders herself not to the poet, but to the representative of active, engaged life. The structure of this poem is clear, but the meaning is not, and in this is found the Symbolist possibilities of lyric allegory. Why Yeldis is transformed from a realistic, living beauty into ideal beauty can only be resolved in the light of the poet's own vacillation between real and ideal beauty, and such conflicting desires are evidenced in most poets since Baudelaire. Lyric allegory of this type leaves itself open to possible interpretations showing the influence on a traditional form by Symbolism because it transforms it into something new.

André Gide's Le Voyage d'Urien (1892) which the author proposed as a Symbolist novel is another expression of the Symbolist allegory of the voyage in search of a poetic land, and of the Symbolist mixture of the rêve and terre à terre sensualism. Gide envisages a voyage from the realm of orderly reason and logical thought:

> Quand l'amère nuit de pensée, d'étude et de théologique extase fut finie, mon âme qui depuis le soir brûlait solitaire et fidèle, sentant enfin venir l'aurore, s'éveilla distraite et lassée.
>
> ...nous promîmes de ne plus nous parler du passé, ni de raisonner sur les choses.[32]

---

[32] André Gide, Le Voyage d'Urien (Paris, 1929), p. 9 and p. 21.

The novel concludes with a return to the world for
after visiting many exotic lands, the expedition arrives
in polar regions beyond which it cannot go. There they
find a man frozen in the ice with a blank piece of paper
in his hand. The reference to Mallarmé seems obvious.

    Our primary interest in the novel, however,
stems from the descriptions in Gide's land of _rêve_.
This novel, like so many Symbolist poems which extoll
an exotic land of pure poetry—far from the ethereal
realm of the blue flower of the German Romantics—is
nothing more than an allegory of earthbound, physical
desires:

> Les matelots se sont baignés dans l'eau tiède...[33]

> Ils se sont baignés dans une eau triste et
> bleue...[34]

> ...une fillette dans un champ d'alfa, brune et
> qui, sous le soleil de midi toute nue, en
> attendant la nubilité, gardait de paissant
> dromadaires.[35]

> Mais à l'horreur de nos refus, nous voyant
> étrangers, ignorants des coûtumes de l'île,
> ces femmes, que nous n'avions d'abord pas
> reconnues, entr'ouvrant leur manteau pourpré,
> montrèrent leur sein peint de rose. [36]

    We should mention in passing another novel of
the Symbolist period, _Bruges-La-Morte_ by George Rodenbach which is the only valid attempt at Symbolism in

---

[33]_Ibid._, p. 39.   [34]_Ibid._, p. 46.

[35]_Ibid._, p. 35.   [36]_Ibid._, pp. 61-62.

the novel form. This work is an effort to use a poetic
method in the novel. It fails because the novel in its
non-poetic function cannot achieve the same thing as
poetry. The work, however, is a fine attempt at Mallarméan imitation, and should be considered for what it
contains of the literary theories of the time. It quite
clearly bears the Symbolist stamp in its atmospheric
presentation, which in itself may be linked to Motif
Symbolism. Structurally the work shares much with the
Symbolist poem. To a central image, Bruges-La-Morte,
is confined, directed, and subjugated every element
of the work, starting with the main characters, the
few minor characters, descriptive elements, similes and
metaphors. The reason for its failure as a prose motif
symbol is found in the need of the novelist to explain
and rationalize upon the symbols he has chosen. It
shares perhaps in a motif symbolism by its more symphonic rather than architectonic arrangements. The
central problem is that of Hugues Viane who chooses
to live with death, makes a brief escape into life only
to find that death has a stronger pull over him, and
eventually succombs to his original state, even more
drastically because of his brief encounter with life.
It is the paradox of death is life and life is death
retold in a concise manner which could only be done
under the influence of Symbolism.

The whole representation of the Middle Ages,
the captive princess, the enchanted castles, fairies,
ghosts, and knight-errants, which appears in such
great quantities in the Symbolist allegories is oriented
toward a sensualism. One is reminded of a Swinburne
making use of the Pre-Raphaelites in England. In many
cases the imagery has been submitted to a process of
synesthesia, but this is done in order to maintain an
ideal realm, to permit the intrusion of the physically
real into a supposed spiritual ideal. It is the cloaking
of earthly desires in a mantle of aristocracy, of
manor houses, gilded ladies, estates swarming with
peacocks and swans, of boat and garden parties, and
perpetual games of love. This ressembles the fallacies

of D'Annunzio in Italy and Valle Inclán in Spain. A
composite view of such poems gives the impression of
a Baudelairian Middle Ages joined to a frivolous, decadent, and Verlainian (of the Fêtes galantes) 18th
century. Some quotations will illustrate these points.
Merrill's "Le Palais désert"[37] is an allegory on the
temporality of love. The image is of a voluptuous
palace setting in which the past is presented by the
sleeping and static quality of the present. Mikhaël's
images are identical as can be seen from his allegories
on unfulfilled love.[38]

---

[37]Plus ne rira, le long des grêles colonnades
La courtisane aux bras lourds de bracelets d'or;
Les pages chamarrés ont fui les esplanades,
Et voilà dispersés, las de leurs sérénades
Les baladins, charmeurs des mandolines d'or.

Les paons sont endormis aux balustrades de fer
Et dans les bassins roux d'où nulle eau ne s'élance
Les cygnes, oubliant leur pâle turbulence,
Rêvent de chants de deuil sous un soleil de fer.
   Merrill, Poèmes, 1887-1897, p. 91.

[38]La dame en deuil, parmi les glycines des treilles
Erre languissamment dans les longues allées
Où des senteurs de fruits et de grappes foulées
Flottent en l'air vibrant d'une rumeur d'abeilles

Ses mains blondes avec une lente indolence
Saccagent en passant des lys et des verveines
Et chaque fois qu'au loin sonnent les heures vaines
Ses grands chiens familiers hurlent dans le silence
   Mikhaël, Oeuvres, p. 37.

Lyric allegories are the cornerstones of poems
treating directly of the poet self-conscious of his
vocation, and evocations of the ideal. Again Merrill
and Mikhaël have the largest number of examples. In
such poems as "Chanson," "Cont," and "Le Ménétrier,"
Merrill establishes a correspondence between the poet
and types which he believes representative of the poet.
Hence, the poet-knight (the seeker of beauty), the
fool (the man of visions and dreams), and the strolling
minstrel (pure music). Only in "Conte" where quest
of the poetic ideal is involved with the Grail legend
is a didactic element present. The riddle of the poem
is revealed in the dedication of the poem to the de-
ceased Mikhaël. The equation between poet and knight
revolves about the purity of the knight in the context
of his pursuit. The poem concludes with a sentimental
image of the dying knight leaving his sword (the poet
his heritage) to those who will come after him.[39] Mikhaël
sounds the same note in a poem on Siegfried in which
the hero senses that he (the poet) is called to greatness.[40]

---

[39]Seul, son glaive flambait sur l'argent de la plage
Afin qu'un futur Preux, surgissant du millier
L'empoignât pour en sacrer son âge
C'est ainsi que mourut le chaste chevalier.
    Merrill, Poèmes. 1887-1897, p. 83.

[40]La mauvaise rumeur des prochaines années
Passe dans les frissons heureux de la forêt
Dans chaque bruit résonne un bruit de destinées,

Et, là-bas le jardin des baisers apparaît.
Et le héros, vaincu par le futur, se livre
A l'ineffable mal d'être grand et de vivre.
    Mikhaël, Oeuvres, p. 52.

Mikhael has composed several long allegorical narratives
on the poetic ideal. In"Florimond", a leader and warrior
has left his friends and now lives in an enchanted castle
with a magic queen. Florimond appears on the balcony
and tells his friends who have come to rescue him to
leave him there for he is happy with his queen in spite
of her cruelties. Florimond is the poet enchanted by
and the slave of an impassible muse. Jean Royère's
"Légende de la Fée Amoureuse d'un Lys" is a more fanci-
ful allegory of the servitude of the poet.[41]A fairy
was loved by all the nobles of the land, but she rejected
them all in favor of a beautiful lily. Trying to caress
the lily, she fell into the pond and was drowned. This
story illustrates poetic dedication to the one eternal
and lasting love, the muse. It also shows evidence of
narcissism, however, for the fairy can be seen as a
reflection of the lily. It finally paves the way to
the great (motif-symbolistic) poems of frustration
where poetry (the muse) becomes identified with virginity and sterility.

---

[41]
. . . .
Or, voici qu'un lys splendide
A germé près du palais
Qu'arrose l'onde liquide.
Dieu juste ! on ne vit jamais
Lys plus beau, fleur plus charmante !
La Fée a senti son coeur
Frémir de joie et l'amante
Tend les bras au lys vainqueur,
Mais la fleur fuit sa caresse
Et la Fée, aux blondes tresses
Expire au sein des flots bleus.
          Jean Royère, Exil doré (Paris, 1898),
p. 41.

A more representative lyric allegory is Mikhaël's
"L'Etrangère," a feeble duplication of Baudelaire's swan
poem. A young woman given mystic caresses by the night,
and to whom the wind spoke of "longues voluptés" went
forth in search of "le fabuleux amant digne de ses baisers." One evening she appeared in a town and offered
herself splendid and nude. The old men of the city
drove her out of town, and the women ran after her and
killed her. A prostitute dragged the dead body over
lily fields. That a story is under the story is hinted
throughout the poem and explained in the dramatic climax.
We know this is a special woman with a special purpose-
to bestow her kiss on the worthy lover. Her arrival
causes the reappearance of things long forgotten, dreams
reappear in the world. Through the reaction of the
ugly mob we know the woman represents beauty or poetry.
She is qualified as "neiges lumineuses," "La bouche
qui savait les mots mélodieux," "la divine morte," and
so on.[42] "L'Etrangère" illustrates the depth obtained
by lyric-symbolist allegories. The concentration throughout this poem is not on finding the abstract term that
each image may convey. The interest is exclusively on
the story, a rather oriental tale of a beautiful woman,
qualified by adjectival phrases referring to an almost
transcendental beauty, who is destroyed by a jealous
(in terms of Mikhaël's day, the bourgeois) crowd. Certain key words as we have just indicated point out the
allegorical nature of the work, but the emphasis while
reading, is on the story, beauty destroyed, and not on
the key.

Mikhaël's "Dimanches parisiens" is his closest
approximation of Symbolism and represents the last
stage of allegory as allegory before it must be transformed into a symbol. Therein, in spite of the explanations offered by the poet, an analogy is brought about
which defies a limited meaning. Until the final explanation the images waver in a lack of definiteness.

---

42 Mikhaël, "L'Etrangère" in Ad. Van Bever and
P. Léautaud, Poètes d'aujourd'hui (Paris, 1927), II,
pp. 28-30.

The poet describes the Sunday stroll of some young
women of Paris, but the images are so arranged as to be
more than descriptive, for the relationship established
between the girls and a wintery Parisian landscape
evokes, as the poet finally explains, the position of
the artist in nature. In strophe 1 the walkers are
dominated, overcast, by a powerful wintery sky.[43] It
is this sky or the atmosphere of the weather which
dominates the poem and creates an allusion of a sort.
To compare these girls and the hostile sky above them
with "L'Etrangère" and the hostile crowd, shows how
superior this poem is, and how, in spite of the didactic
comments, the poem is close to real symbolic ambiguity.
This is effected principally by the constant interplay
of the two images, the wintery landscape ("le ciel
gris lavé d'opale" 1,1- "soleil aux rayons lents" 1,2-
"Poudre d'or vaporeux et pale" 1,3-"sur les promenades
banales"5,1-"les richesses hivernales"5,3-"Et sur
le verglas de décembre"7,3-"Mais le long dimanche,
plus triste/que les plus monotone nuits"8,1-2"jours
blêmes" 9,1-"dimanches longs" 9,2) and the passive doll-
like walkers ("Elles vont à pas nonchalants" 1,4-"Une
senteur de violettes/Mourantes et de blonde chair"2-3,4-
"Elles passent, frêlent, poupées/Aux yeux cruellement
sereins/Adorablement occupées/A bien cambrer leurs
souples reins" 6-1,2,3,4-"Mais le long dimanche/Dans
leurs yeux de froide améthyste/A mis la fièvre des
ennuis" 8-1,2,3).[44]

---

[43]Mikhaël, Oeuvres, p. 5.

[44]Ibid., pp. 5-7.

"Dimanches parisiens" is Mikhaël's best representation of the poet. Here, before the poet equals the walkers and the poet, the walkers, with the characteristics we have just listed, become symbols of a reaction to life which could be shared by anyone. They evoke beauty, self-conscious in a world which is hostile to it. In this the allegory is raised to a universal level which prohibits the singular equations of traditional allegories. Allegory goes beyond this point with other poets, but then it is quasi-symbolic if not fully so, and as such will be considered in the next chapter.

To conclude then, late nineteenth century allegory approaches symbolism by its lyric nature. This means that the image becomes all important and the equations of descriptive, prose-like allegories assume less and less importance. The lyric quality gives greater force to traditional subject matter and reduces the obvious abstraction. The very presence of lyricism, however, demonstrates that the poets are still directed toward an art representative of life at the conscious level. Consequently, attempts to evoke concepts such as ennui, incompletion, poetic vision, beauty, are still held within a concealed realistic frame of rich and sensual images. In allegory the poets are closest to Baudelaire. Symbolist allegory wavered between the real and the ideal, sometimes approaching the latter as in Mikhaël's "Dimanches parisiens." For these reasons, the chief exponents of Symbolist lyric allegory, such as Mikhaël, are not able to produce a poésie pure.

We have so far considered some typical and traditional poetic devices which the minor Symbolist poets employed in their essay at synthesis. We have seen that repetition and refrain remain exterior unifying devices, and that when an interiorization is

achieved, its nature is wavering, emotional and without precision. Personification and allegory attain
the same degree of exterior unity and the added lyrical
note deepens the evocation, but again in a manner which
cannot be controlled. As we shall see in our concluding
chapter, allegory can indeed become quasi-symbolic or
symbolic, but then it is no longer allegory.

       Our attention then must be centered on the image
as such, for it is through the image that the motif
Symbolism exemplified by Mallarmé is developed. Therefore, as a final prelude to our chapter on Mallarméan
imitation we propose to discuss the image under a
double stand of symbolic qualification: the image
working into a single, inseparable element, and the
image as capable of metamorphosis and ambiguity. Such
a division is admittedly artificial, for the former
implies the latter in many instances. We have chosen
this procedure all the same, however, because it can
be made in poetry which is primarily discursive. Because this can be done, it will make clear a process
which is not distinguishable in authentic motif symbolic poems of the hermetic variety. The following
listings make no pretentions to completeness; they are
only indicative of some aspects of image unity among
the Symbolists. Finally, not all of the image unifying
devices are original with or particular to Symbolism.
Certain poetic processes, because they can produce a
unity will be employed anew by the Symbolists.

       The Symbolist poets employed various techniques
to achieve a unified imagery. This can be done in a
simile or a metaphor when one of the elements dominates
a strophe to such an extent that the other element is
minimized or destroyed. A single image by a process
of repetition can bring about through its density a
oneness which seems responsible for the evocation. Two
separate images can be so closely related that they
seem as one, or two separate images can actually be
functionally inseparable. A common denominator can
join two separate entities, or an analogy may be so
close as to effect a very reduced union. Lastly, and

the reverse of the coin, one image can be so constructed
as to be in reality two images.

Pierre Quillard and Francis Vielé-Griffin present good examples of one element becoming so dominant
as to obliterate the other term. In a poem on the
sea,[45] Vielé-Griffin makes a lyrical supposition between
himself and the ocean. In a simile he compares himself
to the rivers of the world which come rushing impetuously
toward the sea. The term of the simile is so developed,
the image supported by such rich qualifying adjectives
that the simile as such is forgotten. Instead the
evocation is achieved through the development of the
river image. Thus the personal lyricism of the poet
is sublimated to the image which is allowed full evoca-
tive power without the constant intrusion of the poet.

Pierre Quillard's "description of the ocean"
in a poem[46] from a series of short poems entitled
"Petits paysages" is an example of the terms of comparison working back on the original subject to produce
a greater evocation. The sea is compared to a pastoral
scene in such a careful manner that one feels but is
not quite sure if the image is applying to land or sea.
It is exactly in this manner and with more intricate

---

[45] Je suis venu vers toi, Mer, comme vont tes fleuves
Impétueux et forts, rongeant le frein des rives,
Tes fleuves triomphants dans leurs courses déclives,
Les fleuves souriants et doux où tu t'abreuves;
    Vielé-Griffin, Oeuvres, I, p. 9.

[46] Une écume de fleurs, blanche et rose, s'étale
Sur la mer onduleuse et mouvante des prés
Où ruisselle le flot des trèfles empourprés,
Tandis que montent vers la nue orientale
Le meuglement des boeufs et la rumeur des blés.
    Quillard, La lyre, p. 189.

developments that the motif symbol poem functions. In
this poem the ambiguity is wholly a matter of structure
and the poem remains fundamentally descriptive. The
foam of the sea is also the flowers of a field, the
moving and waving of the sea is like the same movement
of fields (of wheat for example), and the braying of
the animals and the wind in the fields also aptly describe the noise of the ocean. The terms of the comparison arranged to work both ways destroy the comparison
and make for a single, unified image.

A particular kind of density related to the
repetition technique is found in a little selection in
René Ghil's Voeux de vivre.[47] A series of closely related words give a description of the sameness of provincial life which creates a close unity. Each word
is planned to say the same thing, to reiterate the idea
of sameness coinciding with ennui. Fontainas employs
a similar technique in a poem entitled "Les Heures."[48]

A process common to discursive lyric poetry is
the unification achieved by a term working in two directions at the same time, creating an analogy, and bringing two separate elements together. Jean Moréas has

---

[47]Et, ni ne vivait ni ne mourait la petite
    Ville,—qui se transmet d'une même redite
    d'heures, la quotidienneté qui la limite...
        Ghil, Oeuvres, I, p. 259.

[48]L'heure lassante qui pleure,
    Et l'heure jeune de soleil gai,
    Les heures après les heures
    Défilent lentes où gaies,
    Le long des quais
        Fontainas, Choix, p. 29.

the most common and obvious form of this analogy.[49] He
begins with a description of winter which becomes the
lyric of the poem. The snow falls on the forest which
was so green and alive in the summer (and where perhaps
he spent happy hours with his ladyfriend), and now, as
the snow covers the forest, so it also covers and buries
their love. Merrill more effectively does the same
thing[50] by first joining the two terms and then allowing
them a common fate. His heart, which is like a rose,
has died of sadness, for the ideal, like the beautiful
objects of nature, especially the rose, can only live
a short time. Still more unifying is Merrill's introduction of two terms in a poem which seem separate and
descriptive, only to gain union by the introduction of
a third element.[51] Verbena has wilted in a vase, a

---

[49]Hiver: la bise se lamente,
La neige couvre le verger.
Dans nos coeurs aussi, pauvre amante,
Il va neiger, il va neiger.
    Moréas, Oeuvres, I, p. 30.

[50]Mon âme, en une rose
Est morte de douleur
C'est l'histoire morose
Du rêve et de la fleur.
    Merrill, Poèmes. 1887-1897, p. 149.

[51]La verveine se pâme en les vases d'onyx
Un fantôme de femme en l'alcôve circule
Mais ma mémoire est morte avec le crépuscule
Et j'ai perdu mon âme en les vases d'onyx.
    Ibid., p. 31.

48

fantom woman circulates in an alcove, and the poet
joins the terms when he announces that he is the verbena which has wilted.

Attempting to evocate the horror of the néant
which he feels through the passage of time, De Régnier
allows the image a double development.[52] He is not satisfied with the analogy of the wind to explain his feeling; consequently he imposes on the original comparison
another possible interpretation, the sound of the wind
is the flight of arrows which are being aimed by Time,
the cruel archer.

Rodenbach is able to create very close analogies
while still keeping the terms of comparison separate.
A comparison of the moon with a béguine is illustrative
of this manner.[53] The unity of the analogy is effected
here by the maintenance of a series of comparisons. The
moonlight on the canal is a béguine in prayer, the light
travelling from canal to canal is a béguine going from
parlor to parlor in the convent, and finally, the halo
around the moon is like the white cornette of the nun.

---

[52]Le soir s'endort en du silence que déchire
Flèche ou vent? un frisson perfide que j'entends
Et quelque Archer cruel debout dans l'ombre rire.
De Régnier, Premiers poèmes, p. 262.

[53]Soir de ma ville morte! oh! mes beaux soirs anciens
Où la lune, prenant à son tour l'air chrétien,
Semblait une béguine en prière sur l'eau,
Qui s'avançait ensuite en un grand nonchaloir
De canal en canal, comme dans des parloirs,
Pâle sous la cornette ample de son halo!
Rodenbach, Oeuvres, II, p. 183.

Sometimes there is an interchange of descriptive terms
which strengthens the analogy. The description of the
black-manteled women of Bruges[54] who in their movements
seem like huge black bells, is given a humourous but
nonetheless tight unity when the poet thinks of the
bells as actually being these black-garbed women.

Finally a unity is produced in several poems
of Max Elskamp where he takes what are two separate
terms and forms them into a whole. In "Bon voyage",[55]
an evocation of a holiday train ride into the country,
two images are joined by the phrase "Aux carrousels
des horizons." The poet here actually wants to present a vivid description. Instead of stating that the
landscape, when seen from a moving train seems to
move up and down, as if it were on a carrousel, he sums
it up in a word which indicates the same thing. "Carrousel" is well chosen because of the analogy of a dizzy
movement, and because of its echo of a carefree "dizzy"

---

[54]Des mantes ont passé dans le vide des rues
Oscillant comme des cloches parmi le soir;
On aurait dit, au loin, des cloches de drap noir
Tintant aussi des glas, et peu à peu décrues...

Des cloches ont tinté, graves d'être pareilles
Aux mantes, et d'aller selon un rhythme égal;
On aurait presque dit d'autres petites vieilles
Qui cheminaient dans l'air en robes de métal.
    Rodenbach, Oeuvres, II, p. 176.

[55]Bon voyage, les trains vont vite,
Aux carrousels des horizons
Sautent les arbres, les maisons,
Bon voyage, les trains vont vite.
    Elskamp, Louange, p. 25.

holiday attitude. In another poem from <u>Dominical</u>[56], the
poet in a more serious mood expresses two related, but
separate ideas by a composite image. In order to indicate the loss of innocence, the poet creates an image
of a cabaret; in order to indicate the particular
Christian loss of innocence, he places the tavern on
the hill of Golgotha. By the way, this is a fine
blend of Verhaeren and Claudel, at least as it appears.

As the separated figured elements of a poem
draw closer together, ambiguity and image metamorphosis
becomes inevitable. The synthesis perceived in a flash
of illumination to the poet, finds existence in a form
which will contain such a degree of unity that language
as a divided prose of subject with predication becomes
less important, if not a hindrance to poetic expression.
We have just examined some of the metaphorical techniques
of the minor Symbolists. Let us now regard some examples of the image from the viewpoint of the poetic am-
biguities possible because of the intimate liaison of
the metaphor. A consideration of such occurrences of
ambiguity in poems principally discursive is a fitting
close for the material through which we have been labor-
ing, and a proper introduction to the motif symbol poem.

The most extreme and least effective transformation of image takes place when the image itself is not

---

[56] Je n'ai plus de ville, Elle est soûle
Et pleine de coeurs rénégats,
Aux tavernes du Golgotha
J'en suis triste jusqu'à la mort;
Je n'ai plus de ville, Elle est soûle.
<u>Ibid</u>., p. 35.

permitted a transformation, but is kept discursively
separated by a prose phrase which indicates a possible
union. In Rodenbach's poem on the drowning of Ophelia,
there is a union between the image of the girl's hair
and the image of the floating plant life, but since
he keeps the terms separated, the union can have nothing
but descriptive effect.[57]

The creation of a myth is a step beyond pure
description. Camille Mauclair in "Les Reflets vengés"[58]
explains the existence of swans through a legend: three
young people throw pebbles into a pond in order to
destroy their reflections. When the water settles the
reflections return. Vexed, they try to seize the images,
drown, and turn into swans. Johansen comments: "D'une
manière véritablement poétique, elle est expliquée en
donnant aux cygnes une histoire, en les faisant passer
par une métamorphose qui les met en relation avec l'homme."[59]
This is not a true image metamorphosis, however, for
the transformation occurs in the reproduced legend and
not structurally within the poem.

Rodenbach's poem on time seems to us to be indicative of an image metamorphosis within a discursive
structure. The pendulum of a clock is turned into a
stalactite by an apposition, and the new image is then
so developed. The water dripping from the stalactite,
which produces "la langueur" in the heart, becomes

---

[57]Et ses cheveux verdis, dont la masse persiste
Dans les herbes aquatiques qui leur ressemblent,
Sont si dénaturés d'avoir trempé qu'ils semblent
Un fouillis végétal issu de cette eau triste.

[58]Camille Mauclair, Sonatines d'Automne (Paris,
1895), pp. 68-69.

[59]Johansen, op. cit., p. 177.

minutes dripping from the hour. The drops become black
pearls which roll about a room never to be placed in
order again. The stalactite again becomes a pendulum
up which runs the spider who inoculates the poet.[60]
    Louÿs has given us a drowning poem which is
superior to the poems of Rodenbach and Mauclair, and

---

[60]Songeur, dans de beaux rêves t'absorbant,
La pendule, à l'heure où seul tu médites,
T'afflige avec ses bruits froids, stalactites
Du temps qui s'égoutte et pleure en tombant.

C'est une eau qui filtre en petites chutes
Et soudain se glace aux parois du coeur;
Et cela produit toute une langueur,
L'émiettement de l'heure en minutes.

Collier monotone et désenfilé
De qui chaque perle est pareille et noire,
Roulant parmi la chambre sans mémoire;
Piqûres du temps; tic-tac faufilé.

Ah ! qu'elle s'arrête un peu, la pendule!
—Toujours l'araignée invisible court—
Dans le grand silence, avec un bruit sourd....
Et ce qu'elle mord, et nous inocule!

La peur que demain soit comme aujourd'hui,
Que l'heure jamais ne sonne autre chose:
Un destin règle dans la chambre close;
Un peu plus de sable au désert d'ennui.
      Rodenbach, Oeuvres, I, op. cit., pp. 195-196.

very close to Mallarmé. "Glaucé" (1891)[61] opens with a
description of a beautiful woman bathing in a lily pond.
Her physical beauty is seen in terms analogous to the
description of the water plants, and the effect of the
sunlight (gold and red) upon them. The latter terms
in turn sustain a feeling of death, perhaps triumphal
death, and the poem concludes with the drowning of the

---

[61]
Elle se baigne
Au marais des iris et des grands lys d'eau
Elle se baigne comme un nénufar blanc
Comme un nénufar rouge qui saigne
Elle est tout en or avec des taches de sang
Comme un soleil du soir qui baigne dans l'eau
Miroitante et merveilleuse

Le Marais verdâtre et si lourd d'or
L'étang putride et vert de soir
Est le miroir
De ses hanches
Blanches
O qui chantera l'enfant glauque et d'or
Dans ses mares mordorées

Son fin buste émerge de l'eau
Comme un nénufar chevelu d'or rouge
Ses yeux sont comme deux flammes sur l'eau
Vertes étoiles ses yeux doux d'Asie
Mais sa bouche est un coquillage de pourpre
Et sa chevelure est sur sa bouche
Sa chevelure cramoisie

Ses cheveux longs où sont des algues vagues
Et des crabes verts aux crocs des boucles
Et l'écume des basses vagues
Et des gouttes d'escarboucles
Où les lumières ont des verves
O comme au front des roches d'or
Ses cheveux dissolus couronnés de conferves

woman. Progressively through the poem the woman and
the beautiful plants become more and more inseparable,
and when she has drowned they are one. This would be
only an allegory, in the sense of the Mauclair poem
which we have just quoted, if the poem clearly stated
just such a story. The identification, however, of
woman and plants is consistently made throughout the
poem, in greater and lesser degrees. This is a form
of the motif, a metamorphosis of the basic image by
which woman is plant and vice versa. Parts of the poem
are unfortunately very clear, and we must admit that
the important image of the drowning woman is one of
these. Aside from this blemish, however, a unified
representation of beauty is offered. A oneness is
achieved by a repetition of words, and the working of
these words in two directions, to the woman and to the
water flowers. Despite some of its obvious patterns,
the poem is an example of a description working into a
symbol.

"Iris
Marécageux iris
Mes cheveux sous-marins mêlés d'algues languides
Te veulent triste iris,
Et l'iris de mes yeux."

Voici trouer la frêle eau d'or
Ses doigts luxurieux
Vers les iris, vers les iris
Fleurs droites à fleurir derrière ses oreilles
Larges yeux des étangs, fleurs obscures, bleus iris,
Lèvres molles en fleur sur les eaux
Bleus baisers de la nuit dans ses mains nonpareilles.
Les Poëmes de Pierre Louÿs 1887-1924, Definitive
edition established by Yves-Gérard le Dantec (Paris,
1945), Volume I, pp. 29-30.

Stuart Merrill has created the most ambiguous
and consequently the most symbolic drowning poem of
the minor Symbolists. Unlike the poems just reviewed,
the drowning in "La Mort du Bouffon" is more than just
a description of beauty, for it abounds with implications on the nature of beauty. It is Merrill's supreme
achievement in evoking the role of the poet in his quest
for the ideal. The theme is that of Baudelaire's
"Albatros" and "Cygne." The poem tells the story of an
ugly bouffon, who tired of his jester role at the court,
regards himself in a pond of water lilies and then
drowns himself. By destruction of any consecutiveness
in the descriptive terms of the pivotal strophe, and
by indirect description, Merrill almost gives the poem
hermetic qualities which permit the images to work in
an ambiguous manner. Thus the poem cannot be equated
with any single discursive statement. Two constant
elements interplay in the poem, two images united in
the bouffon because of the tension they produce within
him, and which make a choice mandatory. In the first
strophe the debating elements are introduced, the superficial gay "jeu" of the lords and ladies as opposed to
the pure beauty of the water lilies,[62] the frivolous
and ephemeral beauty of the world, a beauty which flitters
like a butterfly from one flower to another without any
constancy, beauty which is more decor than reality, and

---

[62]Tandis que folle, au vert de la molle pelouse,
La fête papillonne en rondes de décor,
Les nénufars, sur l'eau de la vasque jalouse,
S'endorment dans l'orgueil de leurs corolles d'or.
    Merrill, Poèmes, 1887-1897, p. 61.

the constant beauty which is asleep to the world, noble, proud, and full of mystery. The bouffon, tired of the frivolity, goes to the pond and drowns himself.[63] The suicide is hidden in indirect statement, for the purpose, the meaning of the suicide, is not to be achieved by graphic description of a rather terrible scene, but by a telescoped image. The bouffon regarding his proper image in the pond creates some possibilities: Despairing of his own ugliness he seeks annihilation, but in suicide is the possibility of absorption into a great beauty, that silent and mysterious beauty of the water lilies. In the suicide will be found his true servitude to the only beauty worthy of adoration. Thus he throws away the tool of fools, the "marotte." In the destruction of the bouffon we see evidence of the Narcissus tradition, or rather the bouffon is a new form of the narcissus which stands for the same despair. This brings up the problem of the mirror and identity, the self, and the love exchange. The nénufars are in the soul of the jester and he is in them. In regarding them he is contemplating the beauty of his own soul which is never seen or appreciated by the seekers of superficial beauty.

Merrill's awareness of the transitory nature of human sentiment is deftly expressed in "Bergerie sentimentale," a narrative poem on the ephemeral nature of human love. The over-all feeling evoked in this poem as in others from Merrill's first collection, is the

---

[63] Perclus et se crispant en tristes attitudes
Il mire sa laideur au bord du bassin d'or
Où les blancs nénufars, fleurs des béatitudes,
Le leurrent vers l'espoir du Trône et du Trésor.

Sa rarotte, lancée en l'air, tintinnabule;
Des ronds dans l'eau parmi la fuite des poissons;
Le spasme, une bulle aux lèvres du funambule...
Que lente est cette danse, et que sont ces chansons!
Ibid., p. 62.

sentiment that love is not permanent, that even in its
greatest ascending moments one can detect the roots of
decay. The unity of this poem is found in the action
of the young lady being pursued by a marquis through
an Eighteenth century garden. In this artificial
atmosphere, nature prewarns the end of everything. The
evocation is dependent upon the struggle between two
forces in the imagery, nature struggling with man's
refinements and overcoming them, the ideal crushed by
the real. This is apparent in the fourth, fifth, and
six strophes of the poem[64]where the image is clear but
ambiguous. The girl gently breaks off lilies and roses
from their stems, and sap from the stem, red in color,
runs on her hands. Certain words heighten the effect
and make this image serious. Merrill states that she
plunders with her gentle touch. "Piller" implies disaster,

---

[64]
    Elle pille lis et rose
    Avec de gentils gestes,
    Sans piquer ses doigts prestes
    Que le sang des tiges rose.

    Et de rire ! mais sa joie
    Si pimpante s'alarme
    Et voici qu'une larme
    Scintille à ses cils de soie !

    Car la brise- oh! la malice !
    Lui soupire des choses
    Qui font languir ses poses
    Au bord de chaque calice.
       Ibid., p. 15.

58

destruction. The flower did not resist which it could
have done with its thorns. It allowed itself to be a
victim to the caprice of the young girl. Afterwards,
the girl, in her love making, becomes troubled as a
breeze disturbs her tranquillity. She begins to wonder
at the game of love as she stops at each flower cup. In
a final strophe we learn that her lover has deserted her.[65]
It is now autumn. A listing of the ambiguous elements
coming from this single narrative would be: In autumn,
that is, in its maturity and ripeness, all love dies
following the pattern of nature. The flower gave up
its life on the whim of the girl; it would have died
in the fall as did the love of the marquise. She gave
her virgin love to the marquis who deserted her. The
suffering of the girl is seen in the blood of the flower,
and "calice" of strophe five becomes the chalice of
bitterness along with being just the cup of a flower,
a chalice from which she must drink the bitter dregs,
the consequence of her submission to the god of love.
Finally love and suffering become equated, and the
paradox of the ideal and the real is evoked. Thus is
carried out the warning of the breeze. This poem is
in the manner of the motif poem, none of the images
having anything but descriptive value unless they are
seen as a whole, which then gives ambiguous meaning to
the parts. Merrill has elevated the 18th. century atmosphere type poem of Verlaine, which contains implicitly
the same sense of impending doom as that which over-
shadows the paintings of Watteau, to a metaphysical
consideration of the game of love.

65
>C'était —n'était-ce? en automne
>Est-il mort à la guerre?
>L'écho ne répond guère
>C'était, c'était en automne.
>   Ibid., p. 16.

André Fontainas by a process of Proust-like
association, transformation, and a manneristic circumlocution succeeds in making a single image diverge into several layers of meaning.[66] The poet, walking
through a forest,after a downpour of rain, chances to
notice the raindrops upon the leaves of the trees. The
freshness of the sight refreshes his soul which is
tired of the humdrum existence of quotidian life. The
idea of freshness propagates another discovery. As the
leaves are fresh with rain, they are mirrors which re-
flect the sky, distant and ocean-like. Looking into
the leaves the poet sees himself reflected upon the
ocean of the sky which takes him toward distant islands.
The freshness of the leaves implies the freshness of
new islands to be conquered,in contrast to the life of
the city, and the awareness of mirage present in the
poet's escapism bears analogy to the mirage of the
leaves reflecting the sky. This is almost a motif of
renewal where in spite of the apparent clarity the images
are not so easily disentangled.

---

[66]
Fraîcheur des herbes! un matin de clarté pure
Tout humide des averses de la nuit
Rouvre à chaque miroir qui sur les feuilles luit
Le rêve ancien d'un ciel lointain et calme:
Clairs océans, si j'y bois de feuille en feuille,
Voici me rire l'eau d'un désir; je la cueille
Au vivace millier des scintillantes gemmes,
Et, loin des foules et des villes
Et des vains bruits et des secousses stériles
Où toute ma vie apparaît en éxil,
Je me libère vers les îles du silence !
Ardente proue, une âme s'élance
Fière vers les conquêtes plus superbes
De mer en mer où le mirage
Féconde d'inconnu les anses et les plages:
Là, pure, la vie exulte
Oublieuse, en leur ténèbre, des tumultes,
Et c'est la paix prodigieuse des herbes,
Fraîcheur des herbes !   Fontainas, _Choix_, p. 43-44.

The same phenomenon is discernible in Rodenbach's allegory of the room[67] in which the main image
enjoys a rare ambiguity. In spite of the allegory in
which the poet would see his room as a place of retreat
from life, the mirror image creates real difficulties,
making it impossible to restrict it to meaning the
mirror-lined room of the poet. "Glace" in addition to
indicating the reality, can have the simple allegorical
meaning of a frozen condition, that is, a stable state,
as compared to ocean voyages (better to stay on a quiet
canal than cross the ocean in search of dreams), or it
can go beyond and be the mirror which shows the self
as it is, no longer under illusions. In any case the
image has several potent possibilities if followed, and
one cannot refrain from thinking to the implications
of Mallarmé's Swan or Rimbaud's "Bateau ivre."

Finally the image of the butterfly in a poem
of Rodenbach shows the figure attaining a certain degree of ambiguity, and consequently becoming a motif.
"Les Jardins" is a remembrance of the past caught up
in the image of a butterfly. The butterfly is at one
and the same time a reality (in the pre-poetic tonality),
a personification, an allegory, and a simile. All of
these elements are united in the image of the dead
butterfly. The poet states that the memories of the past

67

Oui ! c'est doux ! c'est, la chambre, un doux port
relegué
Où mon rêve, lassé de tendre au vent ses voiles,
Dans le miroir tranquille et pâle s'est cargué.
Las ! sans plus espérer des sillages d'étoiles,
Et des départs vers des îles, mon rêve dort
Dans le profond miroir, comme en un canal mort;
Et faut-il désirer un coup de vent qui chasse
En pleine mer, cette âme à l'ancre dans la glace?
Rodenbach, Oeuvres, I, op. cit., p. 182.

("Les Jardins de l'enfance aux roses oubliées") are
awakened ("ressuscitent") when something from the past
("dans un vieux livre") is chanced upon. Thus would
be the point of departure in reality for the poet, as
it was for Baudelaire in "Le Flacon." From this he
creates three strophes[68] where the images enjoy a great
dependence. From a simple simile, "the past is like
opening an old book which contains a pressed and dead
butterfly," the poet, by his choice of words and images,
creates a poetic tonality which is one and indivisible.
On the basic analogy is woven the following: Memories
arise, awake, are not dead, nor is the butterfly dead;
he is asleep as were the memories until they were disturbed. As the book is now opened, one recalls when
the butterfly once opened its wings in the rose garden. It was in such a time that youth too unfolded
its wings on the jasmine.

The poems that we have considered in this last
section are all partial approximations of the characteristic device of Mallarmé. They are instances of Motif

---

[68]
Les jardins de l'enfance aux roses oubliées
Ressuscitent parfois dans un vieux livre où dort
    Les ailes repliées
    Un grand papillon mort !

On songe avec tristesse aux arbres en allées
Où le papillon mort, grisé par les chaleurs,
    Ouvrait dans les allées
    Son éventail en fleurs.

On songe qu'en ces jours de floraison première
La Jeunesse, elle aussi, posait par les chemins
    Ses ailes de poussière
    Sur les pâles jasmins
      Ibid., p. 16.

Symbolism in embryo. They represent the highest type
of evocation possible before the poem becomes motivistic through a hermetic structure.

The various poetic techniques discussed in
this chapter are indicative of the maximum unity achieved by most of the minor Symbolist poets. An extensive and detailed study of any of the categories would
certainly exact the precise meaning of repetition,
allegory, and personification in these poets. We have
only tried to sketch some of the manifestations of
unifying tendencies. The purpose of the following chapter, based on all the premises discussed, is to classify
and and analyze the types of Motif Symbol poems found
among the minor Symbolists. Therefore, let us proceed
to an examination of those poems which are directly
in the manner of Mallarmé, and have no link whatsoever
to any kind of graspable allegorism as was the case
with the examples of this chapter.

CHAPTER III

MOTIF SYMBOLISM

What is the process by which poetry jumps from
a discursive, clear, and meaningful style in which the
reasoning faculty can regard, comprehend, enjoy, and
summarize a poetic creation, to the hermetic, non-
discursive poetry which comes into vogue with Mallarmé?
This dissertation makes no claim to answer such an involved and many-sided problem. We had hoped that our
examination of hundreds of poems from the Symbolist
poets would produce sufficient examples of poems partially discursive, partially hermetic, to permit an
actual demonstration of the transformation to the modern form. This was not the case. We have been forced
to conclude that the approach to the difficult poem was
made primarily through the poetic devices which we have
been examining in this text. That is, the lyricizing
efforts of all the minor Symbolist poets, the experimentation with popular forms, rondes, rondeaux, the
resurgence of personification and allegory as revital-
ized poetic forms, the concentration on poetry as music
of Verlaine and his imitators, the impressionism of
Verhaeren and Ghil, the rhythmical considerations of
Vielé-Griffin and Gustave Kahn, are the pre-Mallarméan
essays in the direction of _poésie pure_. A type of poetry in between these forms and the Mallarméan sonnet
is non-existent. The modern poem is born of Rimbaud
and Mallarmé, and some would add Isidore Ducasse, le
Comte de Lautréamont. A poem is either of such complexity or it is not. The evolution toward the modern
poem is apparent in the revival during the last part of
the nineteenth century of the forms listed above, but
a closer link, the evidence of a hermetic-discursive
mixture does not exist. This situation is strikingly

illustrated by the work of Jean Royère. His first volume, Exile doré of 1898, contains many examples of personification and allegory of the type we have considered,
that is, moving toward a poetic synthesis. None of the
poems, however, are hermetic. His next volume, Eurythmies
of 1904 is completely hermetic in the manner of Mallarmé.
How can we explain this phenomenon which is the common
occurrence with all of the minor Symbolists except in
terms of a conscious and deliberate conversion, at least
temporary, to a new style of writing? And so must have
been the process with Mallarmé himself. There are hints
to his mature work in the earlier writings, but the
mature Mallarméan poem is a sharp break with the past.
We would conclude then that the Symbolist poets for
the most part imitated Mallarmé by an exploitation of
traditional forms, and when this no longer satisfied
their creative spirits, they often temporarily or
permanently allied themselves with the modern poetics.
They did not successfully and simultaneously maintain
both forms.

   Thus it is that the primary means, according
to Eigeldinger[1], by which Mallarmé avoided comparisons
and complicated his syntax, the use of the adjective
tel, the accumulation of images without logical connectives (apposition), and the uniting of the two
terms of a comparison by the preposition de, are commonly
used by the minor Symbolist poets (even by Samain), but
without any significance because of the predominance
of discursive qualities which rectify any obscuring
tendencies effected by these devices.

   The hermetic poem is produced by thorough and
radical departures from normal sentence structure, through
the full and constant utilization of stylistic and syntactical devices which minimize or prohibit a rational
evocation, and permit rhythm, sound, and mainly the image
to be the central effective agent. We have already observed some of these methods in our discussion of repetition and refrain, personification and allegory.

---

[1]Eigeldinger, op. cit., pp. 185-186.

Such stylistic turns lean primarily toward a lyric
evocation (for example the <u>media</u> <u>res</u> constructions of
the poems of Max Elskamp) rather than toward a hermet-
icism. The hermetic structure, however, produced above
all by syntactical manipulations, minimizes lyricism
and often makes a veritable Symbolism possible. This
is achieved primarily through the use of hyperbaton
and hypallage. Our examination of the hermetic poems
of the minor Symbolist poets indicated that poems were
often made difficult by the dropping of subject pronouns,
long separations of the verb from the subject and separation of the adjective from its noun causing an ambiguity, the mixing of abstract and concrete terms, a
preference for the general and abstract noun over the
particular, the use of old French forms, the use of
words with an older semantic, the employment of unusual
and learned words, series of dangling participles, in
some minor cases an actual substitution of pronominal
adjectives for pronouns, and finally, the shifting of
tense, a penchant for reflexive constructions, and an
overuse of the infinitive. Some of these tendencies,
for example the masking of verb tense, are very Mallarméan, while others, such as use of an unusual vocabulary,
are not. What is important is the obscuring tendency
and not the achievement point by point of Mallarmé's
devices.

The purpose of this chapter is to examine the
hermetic poems in terms of Motif Symbolism. Therefore
we shall begin our examination with a classification
and analysis of the Motif Symbol poems of the minor
poets, followed by a consideration of hermetic poems
which are not symbolic, but rather examples of an intellectual mannerism in a hermetic structure. We shall
conclude with an evaluation of pastiche-like imitations
of Mallarmé.

The majority of the poets whom we have been
evaluating so far will not be considered here for the
reason that they never wrote a hermetic poem. Starting
at the bottom of the list of modern poets to be treated
are Georges Rodenbach and Gustave Kahn. From the vast

assemblage of their work we have taken two poems which
we believe to be veritable imitations of Mallarmé. Kahn
has few difficult poems. His originality consists in
the elucidation and practice of a French program for
free verse. He certainly alienated himself from Mallarméan Symbolism, and his very concept of poetry precludes imitation. Rodenbach, however, was a conscious
imitator of Mallarmé. Unfortunately as we have seen,
his best imitations end up in personification and
allegory. At least in one poem as we shall see, he was
able to imitate Mallarmé.

Henri de Régnier, André Fontainas, Pierre Louÿs,
and Jean Royère are the four poets of the turn of the
century whose initial essays in the direction of hermetic poetry are directed by the very nearness of Mallarmé. In their works we can expect to find Motif
Symbol poems. De Régnier's encounter with modern
verse was very brief. It is only during the period of
his close relationship with Mallarmé, in the early
1890's, that his poetry shows any influence.

René Ghil is primarily Mallarméan in his very
first sonnets. After his break with Mallarmé, and
his determined pursuit of a universal synthesis, to be
achieved through his theories of verbal instrumentation,
there is little evidence of Motif Symbolism. Ghil's
chief device is a thematic impressionism by which he
attempts to evoke various aspects of life from the
amoeba stage through advanced industrial civilizations.
His work is actually an impressionistic view of the
universe governed by the poet's belief in a naturalistic
and deterministic governing factor. This is tinged with
the altruistic spirit characteristic of early twentieth
century literature. Above all there is a pan-sexualism
throughout his work which well may be the central determining or motivating force. The thematic impressionism of Ghil is best demonstrated in his poems on industrialization. A comparison of a Ghil poem with the
work of Verhaeren on the same subject shows how drastic
the former is over the latter. In Verhaeren as in
Ghil there is a tendency to personify the new machines,

the gods of the twentieth century, but Verhaeren's
impressionism is restrained by a descriptiveness which
dominates the other elements of the poem. Ghil outdoes Verhaeren in onomatopoetic style elements dependent on the sounds of modern industrialization. In
this selection Ghil inserts interjections as expressions
of the foreman speeding the work. The incentives to
work, however, come not from the workers, but from
the tools as such which seem to speak an onomatopoetic
hammer language:

Ho! de la pratique et des Marteaux dialoguants!
chaud, ho! et rouge est le Fer...
L'on doit, à tanguants
haut-le-torse et de haut, l'on doit! le marteler
tel: haut, lourd ! plat-martelons métal et métaux
d'un son des heures: d'un vol! d'un heurt, doit! aller
le vent dans les peuples ventant grand, des Marteaux...
D'un son des heures qui ouvrent l'éveil, allons
d'un son des heures, Tous !

Les marteaux virant en martelant – martelons !-
pour plus d'éternité qu'en l'oeuvre de pierre, et
à tenir les quatre horizons! Ils ouvreront
de haut martelant, les quatre arêtes qu'iront
les métalliques volontés du monde, au haut
de la Tour large, et longue ! 2

The bulk of the poetry of Pierre Louÿs is non-
hermetic. Nonetheless, he was a master craftsman and
while we would find many of his early poems manneristic
imitations of Mallarmé, there is evidence in some poems
and from Louÿs himself that he sincerely essayed Mallarméan Symbolism. Most of his poems, however, are
post-Mallarmé, and in these we are not able to discern
any influence. After his sojurn with Symbolism, Louÿs
busied himself more with prose writings on which his
reputation now rests, and both his prose and poetry
are, as we know, sensual interpretations of Hellenic

_____

2Ghil, Oeuvres, I (Part I, Le Voeu de vivre),
op. cit., p. 151.

or modern civilization.

André Fontainas and Jean Royère are both full-fledged modern poets. Both published initial volumes in which traditional forms are dominant, but afterwards they both became witnesses like Mallarmé, of twentieth century poetry, and like Valéry they are prophets who have lived into the modern day to see the original daring forms become the standard of poetry. We have found many imitations of Mallarmé in their work, but again as with Valéry, these poets often use the new hermetic manner to conceal allegorical, and at times descriptive contents.

The poems chosen from the works of these poets can be called Motif Symbolic poems in the manner of Mallarmé. They are modern symbolic poems because of their hermetic construction and more important because the meaning cannot be made definite as it is in the formula "thought to image." Here the image is dominant and explodes so to speak into ambiguous meanings centering round a basic, existential problem. Because these poems are synthetic, ontological evocations, and not analytical pursuits of particular realities, they are excellent early examples of poésie pure. That is, fundamental human problems are stripped of all particular adornements; the conflicting urges of man are expressed through a basic, ambiguous sign, the symbol, which explains and sums up in its essentialism the inexpressible longings of humanity through the poet's vision, by definition.

We have grouped these poems into categories, each of which is capable of subdivision, and all of which are interrelated among themselves. Such groupings were the natural result of the material. Significantly enough they would also be correct categorizations of most of the poems of Mallarmé, and we hope to make these rapports apparent in our analysis. Lastly, they represent the shift from analysis to synthesis, from lyricism to supra-lyricism, from the particular to the universal. We offer the following classifications:

the motif of absence which is the supra-lyrical transformation of lyric souvenir and regret poems, the motif
of conquest and domination replacing lyric poems of
love and poetic conquest, the motif of disillusion and
hope, and the motif of incompletion and frustration.
There is no trace of any other motif but those enumerated.

Motif of Absence

Absence is a primary concept in the sonnets of
Mallarmé, and is joined to the symbols of incompletion.
We need only think of such sonnets as "Une dentelle
s'abolit," "Tout orgueil fume-t-il du soir," or "Surgi
de la croupe et du bond." The greater artistry of
Mallarmé permits such a fusion. The poems we are
here considering are not in every case of such complexity. Therefore we have separated symbols of absence
and incompletion into distinct categories.

A sonnet of Ernest Raynaud, "Cependant qu'en
un coin de la salle inquiète" is a motif symbol poem
of absence:

Cependant qu'en un coin de la salle inquiète,
Se dédore, avérant un long deuil, en silence,
La chimère du lampadaire, je feuillette
Les images de ma mémoire avec dolence;

Or, par instants, revit la capiteuse olence
Des chevelures que fit miennes la conquête,
Et qu'un souffle disperse, afin que s'en élance
Ainsi que des tisons quelque étoile de fête.

Ce qui n'est plus, la fleur du rêve le décore:
O mirage ! elles sont plus troublantes encore
Tes paroles, Amour ! dès que s'est tû leur bruit.

Et tandis- j'en ressens à l'âme une brûlure!
Que des regrets poignants m'éversent leur salure,
Les astres tracent ellipse dans la nuit. [3]

Raynaud, who is so often classified as a _romaniste_ ,
has in more than a few poems demonstrated his ability
with modern poetic forms. In too many instances, however, his hermetic poems are nothing more than mannered
cochonneries or satiric profiles of contemporary society.
In this poem, the poet is alone late at night in a large
festive room ("salle") where the candles of a sconce are
slowly burning out, one after the other. They are on
the point of extinction. The odor from the wax candles
permeates the whole drawing room. The poet is envelopped
in the smell, and as the light goes out, he becomes
dizzy. The stars in the sky now vividly outlined because of the total darkness in the room, seem to continue their eternal elliptic movements around the sky.

---

[3] Ernest Raynaud, _Les Cornes du Faune_ (Paris,
1890), pp. 97-98.

While in a corner of the unquiet room, the chimera
of the sconce, confirming a grief, in silence ungilds
itself, I sadly turn over the pictured pages of my
    memory.

But, for moments returns to life the heavy smell of
the hair which my conquest made mine, and which a
breeze scatters so that from it may take flight like
    firebrands some festive star.

What is no longer is decorated by the flower of the
dream: O mirage ! Your words are still more troubling,
Love! Ever since their sound has been silenced.

And while-I still feel a burning wound in the soul
from them! poignant regrets shed their brine on me,
The stars print their ellipsis into the night.

This poem is an evocation of the vagueness of
memories, and is effected by the basic image of the
sconce stuck with candles. Late in the night they are
flickering in their last hour, the golden light is about
to extinguish itself (the "se dédorer" is very reminiscent
of Mallarmé), and in their last waverings produce a
chimera of a contourless sconce melting with the darkness
about it. In this vague atmosphere of half-darkness,
the poet turns over in his mind half-remembered memories
of a past love. No comparison is established between
souvenirs of the past and the sconce. Rather it is
the sconce itself which creates the situation. The
poet's intrusion "je feuillette les images de ma mémoire"
is discursive, but not necessarily of an explanatory
nature for "feuilletter" keeps the level of imagery
making of the sconce a book. But the image is not the
single one of the poet alone in his room reading in the
later hours of the night, for he would not just read
in a real book in a drawing room after the guests have
left. This would preclude other possibilities.

The smell, starting from that of a sconce, becoming more and more evanescent, reaches itself the stage
of a chimera, becomes a vague symbol of the past love.
The woman is evoked for a moment in the fading light
and odor of her hair which is analogous to the light
and odor of the candles, first shining, and then extinguished. The tercets contain more explicit material
for there the poet addresses the loved one of the past
and states that the memories which are now so vague are
more troubling than the real experience. He returns in
the last tercet, however, to the symbol. Overcome by
thoughts of the past, in melancholy bitterness fitting
in with the extinguished lights and the overwhelming salty
odor, the poet becomes dizzy, and in this state wonders
about the impassivity of the stars in the sky where
they continue to make their unchangeable ellipses.

The symbolization of the past is effected in
this poem through the image of the sconce which in the
darkness creates a fantom-like illusion. The smell of
the burning wicks becomes for the poet the smell of the

72

perfumed hair of a woman he once loved. This odor is
strongest immediately before the candles burn out, as
perhaps the full love was immediately before its fading,
since possession and fading coincide in human relations
of this kind. The sconce burns out, however, and the
odor disappears. Also the chimera of light and love,
not able to take a precise form disappears. The sconce
with its extinguished triumph of burning candles on its
many branches thus becomes a symbol of the past love
which was a triumphal "étoile de fête", and now too
is effaced. Finally the particular love of the past
is no longer discernible to the poet, the memories have
lost all clearness and order, and his love becomes just
a detached, cosmic phenomenon like the stars, without
any distinguishing characteristics but the one of be-
longing to earthbound nature.

A similar situation is apparent in Henri de
Régnier's long allegorical poem on the past,"Le Fol
Automne", which dates from Poèmes anciens et romanesques, written between 1887-1889. The poems of this
collection are all very long and nowhere in them is
De Régnier capable of the symbolism evident in Episodes
of 1888. Thus there is no transition or development
since both collections date from the same period. The
conclusion for De Régnier and for the other minor writers
is that they could not maintain a motif symbolism in a
long poem. Where the motif exists in De Régnier, is
in the sonnets of Episodes, and not in the long allegorical
poems which accompany them. The answer to De Régnier's
vacillation is not to be found, however, in such exterior reasons. Rather De Régnier had poetic needs
which demanded expression in non-motif forms. I refer
to his romantic lyrical cultivation of the past, his
love of classical antiquity, and the pre-eminence of
these elements in his work. A proper evaluation of
his work would have to consider that despite his
realization of the symbol and its function, his own
lyricism and his knowledge of the symbolic legends of
mankind interplay and fuse with his symbols, and
eventually through a process of lyrical allegorism work

him out of Symbolism and into new modes of expression.

"Le Fol Automne" for this reason is an important work to analyze. If in the sonnets of Episodes we often encounter the poet of Mallarmean imitation, in a poem like"Le Fol Automne" we have a poet who tries to maintain a motif symbol while at the same time expressing pertinent lyrical emotion. The subject is a lyrical one, the evocation of the irrevocable loss of the past. The past in this poem becomes incorporated into an autumnal landscape. The past is a woods in which beautiful nymphs played. For the poet's particular problem, the woods is a place in which he walked with his love.[4] Now that happiness is gone and the poem

---

[4]
Le fol automne épuise aux guirlandes ses roses
Pâles comme des lèvres et des sourires;
Et le mal est d'avoir vécu parmi les roses,
Les masques, les glorioles, les délires !
. . . .
Les Satyres mordirent au bas de ta robe lourde
Les guirlandes d'émeraude et les grappes de rubis;
Leurs dents chaudes ont baisé tes habits,
Les pieds tors ont foulé les traines lourdes;
Ont gambadé devant toi comme des fous.

A l'odeur de forêt de ta chantante chevelure,
Au parfum de vendange de ta chair mûre.
Quand tu passas le long de la mer,
Quand tu passas le long de la grève
Les Tritons blancs t'ont suivie et t'ont chanté
Les chansons de la mer,
Aux échos de la grève;

Et je fus fou comme les Tritons et les Satyres
De ta chair, de tes cheveux, de tes rires,
. . . .
Et je t'ai dit dans la forêt et près de la lame,
. . . .
L'Ode des ors secrets et de l'antique flamme!
    De Régnier, Poèmes 1887-1892, pp. 30-32.

centers on the poet's efforts to capture the past and
his inability to do so. The point of departure in
reality is the autumn leaves, the central and controlling
image. The leaves are leaves and yet they are not. The
green leaves of the summer are in the poet's fantasy
the nymphs and satyrs of the forest. In the summer he
loved and the love is gone and cannot be regained. Also
the enchanted inhabitants of the forest, who were a
part of that love, are fleeing or being blown away by
the wind. The satyrs as leaves and the tritons as
sea shells are natural elements encountered on a walk,
but since the past was also something idyllic, and
with an aurore of fantasy about it, these things of
nature, like his love, are also something else. It is
in the joining of these two elements, the real and the
make believe, that the motif symbol is brought about.
The poet is caught. The dream is gone but it is not
gone, the happy summer is over, the leaves have turned,
but yet they have not turned. The loved one is still
with him, she is also a nymph of the forest who has
left him. In a sense, the poem is the souvenir of an
"Après-Midi d'un Faune," a sensuous summer of life experience in the full season of life, remembered in a
still disturbing non-tranquillity on the threshold of
fall.
    The poem undergoes a true symbolization in the
opening strophes of Part III where the original image
works in two directions. The autumnal leaves burned
fiery colors by the change of seasons are blowing away,
and nonetheless the color inflames the forest. Here
the image is of a mad onrush of colors in a hurricane
wind. The reality is the leaves and bushes in their
fiery array. This image engenders a night image, the
leaves become the torches which are used by the pursuer
of the nymphs to light his path. The poet with torch
in hand vainly pursues a particular nymph whom he had
loved during the summer. The other nymphs of the forest block his way and make possible her escape. The
poet awakens from his dream, it is a cold winter morning, the torches of the autumnal night have been ex-

tinguished, the past has escaped.[5] To summarize the
image of the autumnal landscape as an ambiguous symbolization of the past, we would state that the metamorphosis
takes place in the following manner: In Part I of
the poem, the leaves are simply leaves under the feet

5
Voici luire des torches hautes au bois noir.
La poursuite dénoue aux nuques les brûlures
Des cheveux roux, où vit le feu des astres clairs,
Et les talons légers foulent les herbes mures;

Une torche s'embrase en un bouquet d'éclairs
Ou secoue aux étangs mornes des pierreries
Ou s'enfouit vivante en des antres ouverts.

La forêt vaste éclate en voix vers les prairies
D'où les papillons lourds viennent se brûler l'or
De leur vol nocturne autour des torches fleuries;
Et des rires, abeilles dont l'essaim vif mord
Et harcèle ceux qui les voulurent captives,
M'assaillent dans la nuit si l'une échappe encor;
   Ibid., p. 33.

Celles qui fuyaient dans la forêt sont revenues
Leur chevelure s'effile comme un soir de nues
Les torches de jadis sont mortes en leurs mains nues.

Comme ce coeur saigna parmi ce bois de Faunesses
Entre les mains spoliatrices et chasseresses!
O quel cri d'angoisse, écho des antiques détresses!

Ce fut en des soirs où chantaient les Voix et les Lyres,
Où les cortèges menaient la danse des Satyres,
Et les gemmes craquaient sous les pas parmi les rires.

La flamme, les cris, les rires sont morts et nous-mêmes...
Terne pierrerie à l'or frontal des diadèmes,
Mourez selon les torches noirs en les mains blêmes
   Ibid., p. 37.

of his love, but a comparison creates the possibility
of the leaves as satyrs adoring his love as he did. In
Part II, the summer scene is transformed, the forest
brings out her fall colors, and the wind blows the green
leaves of the summer away. The autumnal image then
transforms itself into an image of night pursuit. The
leaves become torches in the hand of the poet as he
pursues the fleeing nymph who is aided in her escape
by all the creatures of the forest. They deceive the
poet and make him lose the chase since nature does not
foster infantile libido. The poem concludes with defeat: the search is over, the extinguished torches send
pale streams of smoke into the morning air. Those whom
the poet sought are gone forever. Thus the image centers in an autumnal landscape which works in two directions, toward the summer of happiness which is over,
and toward the bleak winter of defeat. The irrevocable
cycle of nature is applied to a fundamental situation
of the human condition.

The defects of this poem are to be found in
its length and in the intrusion of discursive and
allegorical elements. These faults are somewhat avoided
in"Les Vitrages" of Rodenbach:

Les vitrages de tulle en fleur et de guipures
Pendent sur les carreaux en un blanc nonchaloir;
On y voit des bouquets comme des découpures
Adhérant sur la vitre au verre déjà noir.
Mais le tulle est si loin, encor qu'il les effleure,
Et ne s'y mêle pas, en vivant à côté;
Les blancheurs des rideaux n'étant au fond qu'un leurre
Qui laisse aux carreaux froids toute leur nudité!
Et leurs frimas figés, flore artificielle,
Ne font pas oublier aux vitres d'autres soirs
Où de réelles fleurs naissent des carreaux noirs,
Des fleurs que la gelée élabore et nielle,
—Au lieu de ce grésil de linge mensonger—
Songe de fleurs qui ne leur est plus étranger,

Blancheurs où leur cristal se sent brusquement vivre,
Ramages incrustés dans le verre, et brodés
Sur les carreaux qui s'en sont tout enguirlandés,
Rideaux incorporés en dentelles de givre ! 6

The main image is that of the windowpanes surrounded
by curtains with a flower pattern. The problem involved is the absence of more desirable flowers, a dreamy
absence without consolation, perhaps in the sense of
Mallarmé's swan. The windows and the poets are caught
in a bareness of sterility. They dream of a time when
the window panes were decorated with beautiful, esoteric
plants of frost; they desire their own real flowers for
the embroidered flowers of the lace curtain are not as
real to them as the icy flowers formed by the snow and
ice on the inside of the windows. Like the swan the

6

Rodenbach, Oeuvres, I, op. cit., pp. 185-186.

The curtains in tulle and lace flowers
Hang over the windowpanes in a white nonchalance;
Bouquets like cut-outs are seen there
Clinging on the pane where already the glass is black.
But the tulle is so far, even though it touches them
And since it lives near-by does not blend with it;
The whiteness of the curtains being actually only a decoy
Leaving their complete nudity to the cold panes!
And their permanent frost, an artificial flora,
Do not let be forgotten by the windows other evenings
When the black panes gave birth to real flowers
Flowers that the frost modifies and inlays with enamel
                                                   work
-Instead of this sleet of counterfeit linen-
A dream of flowers which is no longer unfamiliar
                        to them (the panes)
Whiteness in which their crystal feels itself come to
                                                   life
Branches inlayed in the glass, and embroidered
On the panes which have become completely engarlanded
Curtains embodied in lace of frost!

window panes would like to be a voluntary prisoner of
icy, virginal-like dreams produced by themselves, and
not mocked by the white curtains. The image itself
does not undergo any metamorphosis, but several meanings
are suggested from it: the vitrages may symbolize an
attempt at harmony with the carreaux, or it may be the
harmony of poetry and music, or the harmony to be reestablished between estranged lovers. In all cases,
despite the fact that there are dreams of change, there
is resignation to fate. "Les Vitrages" is Rodenbach's
closest approximation of Motif Symbolism. Its imper-
fections are the result of repetitious circumlocutions,
and a lack of conciseness. The poem is symbolically
weak and looks like an unwilled parody of Mallarme's
"Dentelle" sonnet.

René Ghil's "Ma Triste, les oiseaux de rire"
is another variation of the absence motif:

Ma Triste, les oiseaux de rire
Même l'été ne volent pas
Au Mutisme de morts de glas
Qui vint aux grands rameaux élire

Tragique d'un passé d'empire
Un seul néant dans les amas
Plus ne songeant au vain soulas
Vers qui la ramille soupire

Sous les hauts dômes végétants
Tous les sanglots sans ors d'étangs
Veillent privés d'orgueils de houle

Tandis que derrière leur soir
Un souvenir de Train qui roule
Au loin propage l'inespoir 7

7
Ghil, Oeuvres, III, op. cit., p. 164.

This sonnet is a new and elevated treatment of the décor-nature romantique poem in the motif manner of Mallarmé. The paysage here has been completely transformed, no exact description is present, and the images are allusive. Instead, a whole symphonic climate of absence is presented as an evocation of the néant of life. It is the country of the "Hollow Men", a paysage beyond despair. This is effected by the negation of the possibility of hope, frozen in the well created word inespoir. The birds of summer and laughter are introduced only to be denied. They do not fly, but sit side by side with death on branches. The idea of the destruction of a past glory is introduced into the second quatrain by the superimposed image of an empire crumbling under a revolution, only to be followed by a stronger denial. In the first tercet the still and horrible present is accentuated by another negation, tears are not allowed to flow lest they indicate hope,

---

My Sad One, the birds of laughter
Even in the summer do not fly
At the dumbness of the funereal knell
Which came to choose the high branches

Like a tragedy of a bygone empire
A single nothingness among the masses
No longer hoping for the vain solace
Toward which the twig sighs

Under the lofty vegetating canopies
All the sobs without the gold of pools
Are watching, deprived of surging pride

While behind their evening
A remembrance of the Train which rolls on
Is propagating despair in the distance

and finally the sound of a train, the only moving and
changing, but rather monotonous object making noise,
and not melody as once did the birds, joins with the
knell of death, and permeates the scene with despair.
This is a static or paradoxically "descriptive" motif
poem. The evocation is brought about exactly because
of the lack of movement and action. By the presentation of a single, almost abstract funereal landscape,
in which each element enjoys an exact similitude of
function, the poem comes to be representative of the
romantic utilization of nature to evoke an interior
sentiment as it could be found in the hermetic poems
of the Symbolists. But the sentiment is always the
same under all kinds of telescoped symbols of absence,
silence, death, ennui, frustration.

Gustave Kahn's "Perdu dans le regret d'on ne
sait quel vécu" is similar to the Ghil poem just
mentioned, but the image tends toward a particulariza-
tion, and moves from the universal:

Perdu dans le regret d'on ne sait quel vécu-
Il susurre en la ville un son d'inexpiable-
Et lasse sous ce morne soleil mal convaincu
    De sa nécessité d'apôtre d'or potable.

Si frêles dans les soirs, si mornes dans les laines.
Villes qui dormez vos ruines à ces lacs,
Sabbats figés d'écarlates aux entrelacs
Des vitraux éclaboussés d'amour pur et de haines
    Rémémorez les fictives scènes.

Sous le lourd faix du temps voûtez les épaules-
C'était aux soirs envoûtés le crime inoubliable.
Depuis, les pieds au feu, un manteau de pôles.

Et passez, et passez sous la lourde relique
    Relique au crâne, aux yeux, aux mains
        Et puis passez
    Aux sempiternels demains
Monotones rongeurs d'éternelle replique.

Dites-nous vos entités
Vos blafardes déités.
Vos robustes mentent leur obscurité
Et puis passez, souffrez, évoquez et mentez.[8]

The poet imagines a magnificent city of an ancient civilization. The city is now in ruins, and the poet speculates on the absence of life. The sun

---

[8]
Kahn, Premiers Poèmes (Paris, 1897), pp. 83-84.

Lost in the regret of I don't know which experience
There whispers in the city a sound of something inexpiable
And becomes weary under this dreary sun, little convinced
of its necessity as apostle of potable gold

So frail in the evenings, so dreary in the wools
Cities which sleep in your ruins on these lakes
Congealed scarlet sabbaths on the crossroads
of stained glass windows bespattered with pure love and hate
    Remember the fictitious scenes

Under the heavy burden of time bend your shoulders
It was in the spell-cast nights the unforgettable crime
Afterwards, its feet on fire, a pole coat

And pass on, pass on under the heavy relic
Relic with skull, eyes, hands
And then pass on
To the everlasting tomorrows
Monotonous rodents of an eternal repetition.

Tell us your entities
Your wan deities
Your robust ones belie their obscurity
And then pass on, suffer, evoke, and lie.

reluctantly shines on this desert city because of the
crimes it has committed. The wind blowing through the
deserted streets is another testimony to the destruction
of the city. The city was perhaps the center of a great
pagan, materialistic civilization, of great riches (by
the way, a bad calque, "or potable," on "eau potable"),
and the weak sun of an overcast day is a pitiful remembrance of that past. The city was built next to some
lakes which are now like dead seas. They do not move,
and the atmosphere of the day casts on them a symbolic
light of love and crime which evoke their once enigmatic stained glass windows in which are congealed
the events of the past, the loves and the hates of the
people who lived there. This city was destroyed because of an unforgivable crime which it perpetuated,
and it must pass an eternity in this condition, without
ever being able to reveal clearly the enigmatic historical situation.

This poem, like the poem of Ghil, is characterized by a unity of description in which the exact
meaning is hard to determine. Each term of the image
is directed so as to concentrate on an evocation of the
horrible act performed by the city, and to which its
magnificent ruins give witness. The city may have just
been destroyed by a superior civilization. Certain
nuances, however, restrict the meaning. The city was
perhaps a center of a pagan civilization. It resisted
the advances of a Christian civilization, may even
have killed a Christian saint. Because of this act,
the city was destroyed. The city nonetheless remained
true to itself; it had acted for what it believed. It
was in the situation perhaps of doing the wrong thing
because it did anything. Its tranquillity disturbed,
it acted and drew the consequences. The poem lacks
the fullness of a motif symbol poem because the meaning
can be so restricted. It is very modern, however, in
that the reader is forced to make such deductions.

Jean Royère is, of course, the imitator par
excellence of Mallarmé, and he is generally regarded
as the only Mallarméan in the short anti-Symbolist
period of the first years of this century. His poem,

"Le blême azur qui dort aux prunelles de marbre" is the best motif symbol poem on absence which we have found, and is a fitting close to that aspect of our discussion:

> Le blême azur qui dort aux prunelles de marbre
> Dans vos yeux d'or mussif, regarde, comme un arbre,
> Vers ce passé lointain où même une clarté
> Ne se distingue pas de son obscurité
> —Entre les pavés gris une mousse si fruste,
> Et mon hoeccéité! —Mais pensais-je, vétuste,
> Devant ce bloc penaud qu'illustre un piédestal,
> Dans une pauvre cour sans phare ni chenal,
> Au lointain frémissant d'une cloche qui tinte,
> Voir palpiter si loin tant de candeur éteinte![9]

The poem evolves from the poet's contemplation of an ancient statue in an enclosed garden, and produces the paradox of absence and the present united in a pondering mind. The statue with its pale blue eyes is a mystery to the poet, for it represents an epoch of humanity which no longer exists. The statue, displaced to a time and place with which it has no affiliation, seems dead to the present and enveloped in its dreams of the past. It represents an ancient civilization of pure and clear beauty which has been succeeded by one which no longer cares for such things. Therefore it is placed upon a pedestal, and put in a courtyard. The

---

[9]Jean Royère, _Poésies_ (Amiens, 1924), (_Eurythmies_, 1904), p. 36.

> The pale azure which sleeps on the marble eyes
> In your eyes of mosaic-like gold, look, like a tree
> Toward that distant past in which not even a bright-
> ness can be distinguished from its obscurity
> —Between the gray flagstones a moss so dull,
> And my haecceity!—But thought I, antiquity,
> Before this abashed block that a pedestal illustrates,
> In a miserable courtyard without lighthouse or channel,
> With the distant quivering of a ringing bell,
> To see throbbing so far so much extinct candor!

statue which had been used to an ocean vista is exiled
in this landscape, and in a way imprisoned. The knell-
ing of a bell in the distance recalls that the statue
is caught in a Christian civilization in which it is
nothing more than a relic, a blind witness of what
has passed. Opposed to the statue, the symbol of
absence, is the pedestal, the moss, the courtyard,
maybe some tourists who regard it, and finally the
poet, who in his scholastic "hoecceité" feels the
naïvete of bygone ages.

   This poem is within a symbolist poetic tradition. We have only to think of Baudelaire's "La
Beauté", and more particularly to his "Spleen Idéale"[10],
or of Raynaud who has a very discursive poem on the
same subject[11], or in a greatly modified fashion, of
the Versailles poems of Albert Samain.

   We have tried to show in the analysis of these
motifs of absence the gradations and variations to be
found within the motif pattern. All six poems have
utilized objects on which the evocation is built, a
sconce, windows, autumn leaves, a Greek statue, two
developed paysages, and through a disciplined control
of these images either made the image as such undergo
a metamorphosis, or placed the image within such a

---

[10] J'aime le souvenir de ces époques nues,
 Dont Phoebus se plaisait à dorer les statues...
   Charles Baudelaire, Les Fleurs du mal (Paris:
Aux Editions de Cluny, n.d.), pp. 12-13.

[11] Avec dans les cheveux la fleur de Ptolémée,
 L'Antinous, au fond des Versailles perclus,
 Se dresse encor, triste d'un culte qui n'est plus,
 Et de survivre à ceux des rois qui l'ont aimé...
   Raynaud, Cornes, p. 18.

hermetic structure that in either case it was difficult
to make it have just one appearance or meaning. The
poems of De Régnier and Raynaud worked out of a typical
love regret lyric, and illustrate how such a particular
subject can be given ontological significance. The same
can be said for the paysage poem of Ghil, and to a
lesser degree, for the poem of Kahn. The vitrage poem
of Rodenbach is Mallarméan in content and performance,
but it lacks the artisanship of Mallarmé. Royère's
poem is completely hermetic, and shows a very original
employment of the Mallarméan construction. In actual
production Royère has established an independence which
frees him of discipleship in the narrower sense of the
word. Let us now examine a related subject, the motif
of frustration and incompletion.

Motif of Incompletion and Frustration

This category is closely related to the pre-
ceding material in so far as absence usually involves
incompletion or frustration. We have separated the
examples, however, because they are distinctly different
from the poems we have just considered, regardless of
this motivistic liaison, and moreover, they are basically
related in their penchant toward a stronger eroticism,
and thus logically fall into a separate classification.
Indeed if it were not for the general implications
arising from the situations involved, if a sexual
symbolism did not involve other areas of the personality,
then these poems could hardly be considered at all.
Contrary to such a situation, because they are motif
symbol poems, and with the knowledge we now have of
archtypal symbols, the following poems illustrate a
most intricate symbolism where the veracity of the
imagery is confirmed by the findings of contemporary
psychoanalysis.

The first poem in Henri de Régnier's Poèmes
anciens et romanesques is above all an allegory, and
because of its allegorical, allusional, and thematic
elements, which too often make the meaning clear, the
poem is not strictly a motif symbol poem. Because of

De Régnier's effort, however, to interpret, expand
upon, and synthesize a primitive legend, and because
of the apparent obscurity and Mallarméan construction
of several of the lines, the poem should be considered
here, and not in the section on allegory.

The poem retells the story of the twelve labors
of Herakles, and interprets these labors as a means by
which he can liberate himself, his household, and his
wife Omphale from some sort of curse. As the poem
opens, Omphale sits spinning at the hearth, in a house
which is permeated with a death-like atmosphere:

1 Je t'ai laissée en l'ombre d'or du vieux Palais
   Où le chanvre roui pend à la poutre rude,
   Assise comme un songe à l'âtre où tu filais,

2 Hôtesse du seuil morne et de la solitude,
   Seule ombre passagère au gel des purs miroirs,
   Que ta face de n'y sourire plus dénude!

3 Du fond des murs épais et des ébènes noirs
   Ton regard m'a suivi comme un oiseau, fidèle
   A mon sang hasardé dans le péril des soirs.

4 Qu'il coule, s'il ne doit fleurir une asphodèle,
   Qu'il coule glorieux dans l'écume et le vent
   Pour toi qui restes en la maison qui te cèle

5 Jalouse seulement de la Mort qui souvent
   —Elle l'imprévue, elle, hélas, une autre amante—
   Baise en l'ombre les lèvres pâles du vivant.

6 Cendres où fut jadis la flamme véhémente!
   Le foyer violet suggère le tombeau,
   Présage à qui ta foi veille qui le démente

7 Tu files à ton rouet le triste écheveau
   Monotone et sans fin comme l'année, Omphale,
   Mais de l'automne renaîtra l'Eté plus beau. [12]

_____

[12] De Régnier, Poèmes, 1887-1892,
pp. 7-8.

Omphale would naturally be sad in the absence of her
husband, but here the atmosphere of melancholy and
death seems also to be coming from a magic spell which
has been placed on the house. Omphale appears almost
as the prisoner of the house. She is not complete in
the absence of Herakles. In the mirrors she is only
a passing shadow. The palace and Omphale, sharing a
common fate, may mean that she is a prisoner of the
self, a victim of introspection, which increases her
feelings of discontent and incompletion in the absence
of her husband. Another possible interpretation is
that Herakles (as lover or poet) must himself undergo
a purification in order to be acceptable to the woman.
De Régnier at least emphasizes the expiation necessary
by choosing a most extreme human condition, the labors
of Herakles. Constantly present throughout the poem

1 I left you in the golden shadow of the old Palace
  Where the retted hemp hangs on the rough beams
  Seated like a dream at the hearth where you spin,

2 Hostess of the mournful threshold and of solitude
  Lonely transient shadow in the frost of the pure mirrors
  Which your face no longer smiling there lays bare!

3 From the base of the thick walls and black ebony
  Your look has followed me like a bird, faithful
  To my blood risked in the peril of the evenings.

4 May it run, if it does not make flower a daffodil,
  May it run glorious in the foam and the wind
  For you who remain in the house which conceals you.

5 Jealous only of death which often
  —She the unforeseen one, she, helas, another lover—
  Kisses in the shadow the pale lips of the living

6 Ashes where was formerly the passionate flame
  The violet foyer suggests the tomb,
  Omen to which your faith belies, keeps watch.

7 You spin at your wheel the sad hank
  Monotone and endless like the year, Omphale,
  But from autumn will be born again a more beautiful
    summer.

is Omphale and Herakles' conviction that they can
change this fundamental situation, and equally present
is the feeling that despite the optimism of Omphale,
despite the deeds of Herakles, which for a moment may
make to flower a daffodil, the incomplete situation
will remain, and Omphale and Herakles will have to
submit to their unhappy fate.

The poet turns his attention to the labors of
Herakles, and after evoking them, states that they
have removed the spell[13]. In strophe twenty, De
Régnier makes a faint echo to the Virgin in the Apoca-
lypse to reinforce his images of the conquering Herakle.[14]
The poet announces that a great peace fills the earth,
"De grandes fleurs ont refleuri la terre aride"[15]. He
ends the poem, however, with a reference to the death
of Heracles, indicating that any resolution of the
problem was temporary,[16] that eventually the situation

---

[13]Le mal mystérieux agonise et trépasse;
Les douze Epreuves ont purgé l'ombre et voici
La massue et le glaive au poing nu qui terrasse;
  Ibid., p. 9.

[14]Il a foulé le mal de son pied nu qui pèse
Sur la gorge étouffée et la gueule qui mord
Jusqu'à ce que le dernier cri râle et s'apaise
  Ibid., p. 10.

[15]Ibid.

[16]Et si son coeur, hélas, mordu par la chimère
Durant le dur travail de ton nom illustré
Elude sa tristesse en quelque cendre amère,
Laisse le bûcher d'or fumer au ciel sacré!
  Ibid.

ordered by fate in the opening strophes of the poem
would have to return.

This poem is like a motif, at least in the
opening strophes which are superior to the remaining
allegorical elements, and which contain all the necessary elements of the poem. Moreover, the evil to
be overcome, the exact nature of the difficulty is
never defined, which leaves room for interpretations.
This is also the situation in the legend outside the
poem, despite any explanations offered. Finally, the
syntax is often difficult. This allows the individual
words to form symbolic units which take precedence
over any logical relation the words have to each other.

André Fontainas and René Ghil have created
motifs of incompletion which are not discursive or
allegorical. A certain sensuality is discernible
across the work of both these poets, and in the following examples they elevate this characteristic to a
real symbolization.

Fontainas' sonnet, "Le Parc sentimentale" is
a pastoral motif, an invitation to life and love
through nature:

O brises et baisers des brises, pour vos lèvres
Palpite en nudités royales la splendeur
Des glaïeuls et des lys, et s'affine une odeur
De verveine frissons infinis et mièvres.

Rubis clairs scintillants ignorés des orfèvres,
S'est offerte vers toi, frôleuse, la candeur
de quelles tiges! et tu ris, Enfant Rôdeur
Qui pais en nos jardins le troupeau de tes chèvres.

Pâtre, de la pelouse verte où tu t'endors,
Un thyrse ondule vers ton rêve ses bras tors
D'enthousiaste ardeur pour quelque amour antique,

Tu frémis! et voici des buissons à tes yeux,
Nue et ses cheveux blonds ceints du myrte mystique,
Se dresser la Vivante au regard radieux. [17]

---

[17]Fontainas, Choix, p. 21.

A shepherd wanders into a verdant garden. He is de-
lighted by the beauty about him, and resting on the
ground, he falls asleep. While sleeping he dreams of
participation in life, of being loved. Awaking, he
finds his dream come true, for standing before him is
the reality, a young woman inviting him to love.
        The evocation comes about through a metamor-
phosis of the descriptive elements. The garden is
described in terms of full life, desire, and promise.
The breeze, filled with sweet odors is prepared for
the shepherd's lips. The flowers are opulent, almost
sexual, even phallic. They tease the shepherd as he
brushes against them; they bid him welcome and almost
dare him to become part of life. The shepherd has
passed into the realm of love. Falling asleep in this
atmosphere which is full of the rich beauty of over-
ripe, sweet smelling flowers, the garden scene invades
his dreams which become infected with the atmosphere.
The "tige" of the flowers becomes transformed into the
erotical symbol of Bacchus, the Thyrsus staff. When
he awakes, the dream and the reality fuse into one as
a young girl, perhaps the flowers or rather a shepherdess,
stands waiting before him.

O breezes and kisses of the breezes, for your lips
The splendor of the gladiolus and the lilies
flutters in royal nudities, and an odor of verbena is
busy to refine infinite and teasing thrillings

Like sparkling clear rubies unknown to the goldsmiths
was offered you, grazer, the candor
of what stalks! and you laugh, child roamer
who nourish in our gardens the flock of your she-goats

Shepherd, from the green lawn where you fall asleep
A thyrsus undulates its wreathed arms toward your dream
with an enthusiastic ardor meant for some antique love

You shiver! and here there rises from the bushes before
your eyes, Nude and her blond hair braided with a mystic
myrtle, The Living One with a radiant look.

The theme of incompletion is found in abundance
in the work of René Ghil. It appears in every section
of his work, which he claims is a synthesis of the
human experience. Since the whole work revolves about
the successive evolutions of mankind, poems on Man's
harmony and lack of harmony are to be expected. The
work as a poetic whole has as many faults as the philo-
sophy behind it. It tends to obscurity, and at times
is painfully ridiculous, as for instance, in the ode
to phosphorus. Ghil was obsessed with the idea of
evoking man in his creative processes, and while many
of his poems on that subject are closely related to a
naturalistic—impressionism, he is still able to write
poems of greater artistic unity. The following selection
from Le Geste ingénu is a fitting example:

De vêtures aux plis que n'ont palpés de doigts-
unanimes de pas et soeurs en des guirlandes
viennent en solitude les Vierges, sans rois
apparus à l'étang des miroirs sans girandes....

Que venaient de longtemps les danseuses d'orgueil
tranquilles et parmi l'espoir d'un apogée
qui monte à donner l'âme de splendide deuil
à l'ampleur de seuls lis en leurs mains érigée:
divulguez-le, depuis les soirs évanouis!
ô large tourment d'ouvrir l'Espace,

                                        de phare
versant sur l'Aventure auguste des Minuits
une dispersion de la nouvelle rare !
Un âge de savoir qui sur soi se taisait
de longue sûrete vêt le pèlerinage
allé vers la région d'Elles-mêmes, qui s'est
ouverte de leur signe ample et sans voisinage

que le sens d'Elles su ne sera dévoilé !. . .

Aussi longtemps qu'un soir sonnera ses venues-
et que lui survivra sur l'onde d'un seul lé
la genèse d'émois de phare dans les nués:

qui venaient en levant la vertu des lis d'air
un passage augural et son songe de gloire
muet geste en sourire à des phases d'hier-
divulguez-le, plus loin qu'une humaine mémoire !

vent de lumière, éteint dans l'avenir de moire...[18]

After having shown the harmony which exists between
male and female, Ghil creates this poem on women who
did not or did not want to find a mate. Here he
successfully creates a feeling of incompletion by a
combination of sound and stylistic devices, plus the
interlocking of an imagery which works in several
directions. The selection contains many alliterations
and echo elements; the connectives are ambiguous, rough,
and the sentence is almost violated by the non-harmonic
joining elements; the cacophonies seem overdone (...
sûreté vêt le pèlerinage), there is an overuse of vo-
catives, and a discernible use of nasals. These elements provide a secondary unity to the imagery which

---

[18]Ghil, _Oeuvres_, I, _op. cit._, pp. 90-91.

Like clothes with folds which fingers have not touched
equal in step and sisters by their wreathes
come the Virgins in solitude, without kings
appearing at the pond, mirrors without waterspouts...

From what remote a time were coming the proud dancing
                                                  girls
Peaceful and amidst the hope of an apogee
Which surges forth to give the soul full of a splendid
                                                  sorrow
To the amplitude of the only lilies raised in their
                                                  hands:
Divulge it, since the evenings have vanished!
O terrible tormenting drive to open the Space
Pouring forth from the lighthouse on the august
  Adventure of the Midnights
A dispersion of the rare news !
An age of knowledge which on itself remained silent

is working in different directions to indicate that
the virgins may be virgins somewhat against their will.
The image actually evokes the procession of a group of
virgins. Their clothing is associated with the habit
of nuns ("De vêtures"), and it is announced that these
women are pure ("aux plis que n'ont palpés de doigts").
A mournful procession, however, takes place, since it
consists of those who have separated themselves from
life. Each element is designed to indicate a nun-like
exile from men. At the same time the image is qualified in such a way as to indicate that the renounce-
ment of life is not entirely pure or voluntary. The
virgin-queens march in solitude without kings; the
mention of the male element implies unavowed desire.
As they pass a lake, the lake becomes a mirror in
which there is no reflection of kings, of men, because
they are marching alone. Their single reflection in
the pond suggests absence and incompletion, as the
pond itself is incomplete without waterspouts, the
always fructifying element of water basins. Both
virgins and pond are undisturbed vessels. The next
strophe opens with a desire for the peaks of virginal

---

with a long surety dresses the pilgrimage, a procession which walked toward the region of themselves,
which opened itself at their full sign wide and
without any neighborhood, so that the meaning known
by them only will not be revealed! . . .

As long as an evening will announce its comings
and that will survive it on the wave of a single
breath-measurement, the genesis of lighthouse-like
emotions in the skies:
Which were coming to remove the virtue from the lilies
of the air —an augural passage and its dream of glory
a mute gesture in smiling at the phases of yesteryear-
Divulge it, farther than a human memory!
wind of light, extinguished in the future of the
 watering...

94

pride ("parmi l'espoir d'un apogée"). The "deuil" is
"splendide" because there is subjectively complete
resignation, and the lilies which the virgins carry
become at the same time their mysterious symbol in
their unyielding rigidity. By making each segment
of the image pull in two directions, toward virginity,
and away from virginity ("deuil"), Ghil establishes
a veritable motif situation, an inextricable état d'âme.

The selection has other elements, however,
which indicate that the poet may not be satisfied with
his designation of the virgins. He seems to have a
faint idea that perhaps the virgins are en route to
a great and pure conquest. Without any disturbance
("sans voisinage") the virgins march toward the regions
of themselves, that is, they desire to undergo an
interior purification in order to reach a Mystical
state. The capitalized E in "Espace" shows mystical
desire not as frustration, but as a real and positive
situation. Ghil then, in spite of his penchant to
negatively interpret virginity, sees the possibility
of a positive maidenhood, a new reason (to him) for
virginity, a reason which should henceforth be always
known.

Our best example of the motif of incompletion
comes from an early sonnet of Ghil (1886). The influence of Mallarmé is more perceptible in this poem
than in the mature work of Ghil where his symphonic
expansiveness is detrimental to the symbol. "Mais
leurs ventres" is an excellent example of a refined
hermetic structure with a very close interlocking of
images:

Mais leurs ventres, éclats de la nuit des Tonnerres!
Désuétude d'un grand heurt de prime cieux
Une aurore perdant le sens des chants hymnaires
Attire en souriant la vanité des Yeux.

Ah! l'éparre profond d'ors extraordinaires
S'est apaisé léger en ondoiements nerveux,
Et ton vain charme humain dit que tu dégénères !
Antiquité du sein où s'épure le mieux.

Et par le voile aux plis trop onduleux, ces Femmes
Amoureuses du seul semblant d'épithalames
Vont irradier loin d'un soleil tentateur:

Pour n'avoir pas songé vers de hauts soirs de glaives
Que de leurs flancs pouvait naître le Rédempteur
Qui doit sortir des temps inconnus de nos rêves.[19]

At dawn the sky rolled with thunder as if some
god in the heavens or on the earth were about to witness
a great storm, with flashes of lightning. The use of
ventre seems ambiguous: is there involved the sigh
connected with wombs in birth pains, or is it the flashes of coquettish bosoms far away from their real destiny. The first interpretation is immediately destroyed
for after the terrible agnoizing hours of the night, a
beautiful dawn, now symbolizing the young bosoms as
conscious of their attractiveness, but not ready for
their destiny of procreation ("Désuétude d'un grand
heurt..."), for productiveness ("Une aurore perdant
le sens des chants hymnaires), is offered to view. The

---

[19]Ghil, in Van Bever and Léautaud, op. cit.,
I, p. 98.

But their wombs, flashes in the night of Thunderstorms!
Desuetude of a great collision with the primal skies,
A dawn losing the meaning of the hymnal songs
Attracts smiling the vanity of the Eyes.

Ah! the profound scattering of extraordinary golds
Lightly is pacified in nervous undulations,
And your vain human charm says that you degenerate!
Antiquity of the breast on which is purified the best.

And by the veil with the too undulating folds, these
Women
Enamored of the mere appearance of the nuptial song
Go to irradiate far from a tempting sun:

For not having thought towards the solemn evenings of
the swords
That from their sides could be born the Redeemer
Who is to come out of the unknown times of our dreams.

sun rises (second quatrain) and the brilliance of the
original aurore seems quieted down, were there not
nervous undulations. At this point, the dawn image
is given its full purpose. The question is posed:
Does a blossom exposed to the sun degenerate, although
in a process of maturation, or is the sun a purifying
and rehabilitating agent for the better. The role of
these natural forces is determined in the tercets where
the answer to the problem is given. In this sun walk
some women who are radiantly beautiful in themselves.
They are fertile and ready for marriage and creation.
They are, however, of the same nature as the dawn. Prepared to create, they reject creation because of their
vanity. They prefer to be just beautiful, like the
dawn, and not productive. A final ironic twist is
given to the sonnet. These women have rejected motherhood when the possibility existed for their wombs to
carry the Redeemer of the world. At the Annunciation
they would have said no to the angel. They prefer an
ephemeral beauty to the deformations of their bodies
which motherhood would require.

       This sonnet is a very clear illustration of
the operation of the motif symbol poem. The evocation
is only possible through the intimate linking of these
images, which are meaningless unless they are joined
or rather telescoped. A few examples will show how
the parts of the image cross. The nature description,
a storm in the sky in the last hours of darkness before dawn, is evoked in the very beginning of the poem
in terms of human possibilities of creation or pride.
In the same description, dawn is presented in terms of
a vain, coquettish woman, and is destroyed as the day
advances. The introduction of the women in the tercets constantly refers back to the quatrains. The
women are also vain ("Attire en souriant la vanité
des Yeux"), and eschew their duty ("Amoureuses du
seul semblant d'épithalames"), and only pretend to be
marriageable. Their beauty refuses to expose itself
to the possibility of fertilization in the sun, so
they take shelter under veils which keep out the rays

of the sun. The rays of the sun which are dispersed
across the countryside become transformed into a
phallic symbolic sword ("glaive") which in itself
explodes into several meanings. The women have re-
fused the sword of life which they interpret as a
sword of death (giving birth being a risk), not reali-
zing that by productivity, the dream of an ideal, sym-
bolized in the Ancient Hebrew rêve of a Redeemer,
could have materialized. By this sword, the night of
the world could have been bannished, thanks to their
cooperation: Their child might have been a peace maker,
a healer, a helper of mankind.

There are exterior similarities between elements of this poem and two sonnets of Mallarmé. These
are not of real significance, but all the same indicate a possible unconscious imitation. The second
tercet of Ghil's poem recalls the second quatrain of
"Le vierge, le vivace et le bel aujourd'hui," and to
a lesser degree the second line of the second tercet
of Ghil echoes Mallarmé's "Filial on aurait pu naître"
of "Une dentelle s'abolit."

Poems on incompletion and frustration form a
minor part of the whole Symbolist production. They
have an exaggerated importance in the work of Ghil.
The subject is a fundamental paradox of life, however,
and is present in the poetry of Mallarmé (Hérodiade
for example), of Valéry (La Jeune Parque), and was
to be expected in the poems of the minor Symbolists.
With Mallarmé, the frustration motif turns more on
the subject of poetry, and it is the same with Valéry
to a lesser degree. The major poets and the poems
of the minor Symbolists here reviewed show that it is
a proper subject for poetry because of its concomitant
implications for both poetry and life, for the ideal
and the real.

Motif of Conquest and Domination

I have remarked that the motif of absence is
not too different from the motif of incompletion and
frustration. The same may be said for the poems to
be analyzed under the category of conquest and domination; it is in fact the other side of the same thing.
Man struggles against his solitude, his sterility, and
through ambition seeks to remedy the split in his personality. Opposed to the swan frozen in the ice, the
march of the virgins, the arid and wasted countryside,
are those objects which come to symbolize man's desire
and effort to control his destiny, to dominate, and
to produce. It may be a matter of domination in love
or the breaking of the chains which impede poetic
creation. These are the two main subjects for the
motif symbol poems of conquest and domination. Need-
less to say they transcend their particular theme and
arrive at a universal symbolization. To say with Freud,
if the earlier examples were concerned with the libido,
these ones are concerned with the complex of ambition.
The steps necessary to achieve this type of
symbol may be readily observed if we commence by comparing two conquest poems of Henri de Régnier. His
Tristan sonnet attempts to portray the love of Tristan
and Iseult by a utilization of the objects about them:

Le blanc cheval marin qui cambre son poitrail
D'ivoire mat et semble hennir à la proue
Sous le fouet aigu des écumes s'ébroue,
Et Tristan vêtu d'or s'accoude au gouvernail.

Sous la tente qui s'ouvre en roideur de camail,
Au souffle rauque de la mer qui la secoue,
Iseult, pâle, dont la guirlande se dénoue,
Tressaille au choc de ses pendeloques d'émail.

Profond comme la mort et l'amour qui l'a prise
Le murmure des flots l'épouvante et la grise
Et le philtre a rougi les lèvres du Héros.

Terre! et des chefs casqués d'un cimier d'ailes noires
Dans la corne sonore et torse des taureaux,
Sonnent pour son accueil du haut des promontoires.[20]

A rapport is made between the personages and the objects. The first quatrain evokes an arched horse, the
figurehead of the ship on which Tristan is bringing
Iseult to King Mark. The horse is neighing at the
waves, which jump about him. Tristan is kneeling at
the helm guiding the ship through the sea. Iseult,
under her tent, is shaken by the ship's movement
through the rough waters, and a wreath of flowers in
her hair has come untied. The sound of the waves
which is as deep as death and their love frightens her.
As they reach land, the leaders of King Mark, whose
helmets bear crests of black wings, blow into sonorous
and twisted bulls' horns to bid her welcome.

The images in this poem are all united to produce an evocation of conquest and feelings of impending
doom. The horse figurehead on the prow of the ship,
the ship as the horse of the waves being an old Norse
and Anglo-Saxon Kenning, is a male sign in conflict
with the sea through which it ploughs. Tristan is
the man of action who guides the ship, and the horse
here is a figured extension of him, the ship being
actually called with another kenning "rider of the
waves." The storm on the ocean indicates the collision
of the male and female forces localized in Tristan
and Iseult through the potion. Iseult's passive reaction to the sea symbolizes her inability to refuse
Tristan, and the untying of the garland, the loss of
her virginity. At the same time the sea storm represents the internal turbulence and tensions of the
lovers, the guilt they share, and the future encounters
with King Mark. The male symbol is resumed again in
the last strophe, the horse is replaced by the horns
of a bull. As the legend is known, the poem can only
be a very good allegory. If De Régnier had not particularized, and had the structure been hermetic, a
first rate symbol poem could have been the result.

[20]De Régnier, Premiers Poèmes, p. 284.

Such is the case with "Au sommet de la proue"
which is perhaps De Régnier's finest motif symbol poem:

Au sommet de la proue où veille un bélier d'or
En spirales dardant le défi de ses cornes
S'évanouirent au vent d'Est les gammes mornes
Dont le Pilote berce un regret qu'il endort;

Les écumes des mers sont des toisons encor
Qu'éparpilla le saut astral des Capricornes.....
Et c'est la vieille vie où s'accoudait aux bornes
Le bucolique rêve en un autre décor;

L'air pastoral évoque un soir où l'on débrouille
L'écheveau d'hyacinthe au bois de la quenouille
Et le thyrse du pampre crispé qui l'étreint,

Car ce joueur, enfant, incisa les écorces
Et fut pâtre, avant de guider au port lointain
La proue où le bélier darde ses cornes torses. [21]

The poem seems an evocation of triumph over defeat,
and of male over female. In the first quatrain a
ship is seen at sea guided by a half-awake shipmaster.
In the turbulent waters, the golden ram figurehead at
the prow of the ship seems to be defiantly bucking the
water. The East wind is so strong that it outdoes the
melodious songs of the pilot, sad songs concealing some
pain. In the second quatrain the foam on the waves is
represented as being the fleece of sheep which the stars
of Capricorn - sheep and rams themselves according to
their Latin name - scattered about in the ocean. The

---

[21] Ibid., p. 158.

At the summit of the prow where watches a golden ram
Hurling the defiance of its spiralled horns
The mournful tones faded away in the Eastern wind
By which the pilot rocks a regret that he lulls to
                                              sleep

last line of the second quatrain forms the transition
to the tercets. The ship guide was once a shepherd
who used to guide sheep, and this sea situation is
a reminder and remainder of the old mythic life in
which on the corner stones lay in waiting (for the
possibly passing nymphs) the bucolic dream (of the
faunes) in a bucolic, and not a maritime setting. The
first tercet, through the transition of the second
quatrain, has an analogous task. A pastoral scene is
evoked, but the exact meaning is difficult to construe.
From the distaff, a tool used in spinning, is disentangled
hyacinth, and the tightly-clinging vine branch is disentangled from the thyrsus. This brings to mind a
country scene, women engaged in feminine occupations,
such as spinning, but here only some joyful and youth-
ful task, and the followers of Bacchus gathering in
the grape harvest. The image of the staffs relates to
the "cornes" of the "bélier"; the distaff, the sign
of the female, is put in close relationship to the
thyrsus, the male sign, the staff of Dionysus and the
satyrs. The symbol may be particularized to a sexual
meaning or kept on a general plane indicating dominance.
In the second tercet, the pilot, the same Dionysian is
recalled ("regret" of strophe 1) as the shepherd who

The foams of the seas are still fleece
That the astral jump of the Capricorn strewed about
And it is the old life where at the limits leaned
The bucolic dream in another decor;

The pastoral air evokes an evening when is disentangled
The hank of hyacinth on the wood of the distaff
And the thyrsus of shriveled vine branch which clasps it,

Because this player, a child, notched the barks
And was a shepherd before guiding to the distant port
The prow where the ram hurls his twisted horns.

tapped the barks of trees in a time prior to his guiding the ram-decorated ship through the flock of waves
to the far away port.

De Régnier works on many levels in this sonnet,
and they cannot be viewed separately, for the tonality
of the poem is dependent on their very interdependence,
(ram-corne-fleece-capricorne). One must therefore conclude that this is a motif symbol poem in which the
image explodes into various levels of meaning. Several
interpretations suggest themselves. The poem may be
seen as a voyage poem. One can see allusions to the
legend of the golden fleece, Jason and the voyage of
the Argonauts, great masculinity determined to conquer
the desired prize. It may even be seen as the symbolist voyage to Cythera, the pilot being also a kind of
Cupid in relation to a Dyonysos-Faune. Capricorn, a
sign of the zodiac is another possible starting point,
the ram, the dominant male symbol as presented in the
horns of the ram who conquers the female. This symbol
would be intertwined with the voyage symbol. This
recalls the story of Zeus in the form of a bull, who
carried off Europa, which is used also by Góngora at
the beginning of his voyage poem Primera Soledad I.
The ram seems to push the ship through the waters
(female sign), dispersing the waves. The ram symbol
jumps from the ship up into the heavens, and becomes
part of the constellations which act on the waters.
The ram is also thought of in terms of his natural
habitat, in a pastoral scene from which the same
essence may be extracted. Finally a weaker symbol may
be seen in the image of the distaff and the thyrsus.
The distaff comes to represent the female, and the
thyrsus the male. With this staff Dionysos follows
the nymphs, disentangling the brush for this purpose.
This seems a more suggested image but is to the point
to continue the erotic atmosphere.

The image of the pâtre resumes all previous
images and is essential to the unity. The shepherd
dominates his flock, the ram dominates the sheep,
the thyrsus is a sign of manhood, a masculine sign in

a dionysian rite, the shepherd is a ship captain who
successfully gides his ship to a distant port, the ram
forces its way through the fleece of the waves, the
thyrsus dominates the distaff as the faune dominates
the nymphs, the staff is used by the shepherd to herd
his sheep, and the staff is the horns of the ram.

Pierre Louÿs' "Diagonale" (1891) is a poem of
tranquillity after a storm of passion in which two
lines of images are crossed in the motif manner:

1 En vos prunelles iridées
  Matutinal s'évanouit
  Le tourbillon des sens de nuit,
  L'essaim des bêtes mal bridées,

2 Chimères de gueules qui font
  Tresse aux tiges sous les corolles,
  De fantastiques flammeroles
  En barre sur le ciel profond;

3 Griffons d'or aux ailes de sable
  Au vol éployé sur l'écu
  Parmi les lys ayant vécu
  Dans le seul songe efflorissable

4 Poissons de sinople et d'argent
  Eclos en torses de sirènes
  Licornes bronchant sous les rênes,
  Et, la pointe à terre, chargeant;

5 Stryges dont le pied sec s'empierge
  De népenthès et de lys d'eau,
  Tout s'envole comme un rideau
  Sur une limpidité vierge.

6 Et, péchés d'aube aux yeux malsains,
  Fièvre des cernures livides
  Forme en péril des corps avides
  Qu'un vent suspend au cap des seins

7 Double rêve qui s'écartèle
  De pourpre dans l'or du blason,
  La fuligineuse toison
  Brochant sur l'étreinte immortelle,

8 S'apaisent. Mais l'étrange essor
Psychique étend son envergure
Innombrable où se transfigure
Un vol d'images sur champ d'or,

9 Et l'aube fait fleurir idées
Le tourbillon des sens de nuit
Qui s'éclaire et s'épanouit
En vos prunelles iridées.[22]

Unfortunately the images are not condensed enough to
create an ideal symbolization, but the discursive
separation effected by the poet in the introductory
and closing strophes, and the descriptions of the dream
in strophes 2-7 do not destroy the evocation.

In the morning light a lover looks into the
tranquil and iridescent eyes of a woman, and is amazed
that they in no manner whatever express any of the
torrential passion of the night. The "prunelles
iridées" become the agents then for the symbolization
of tranquillity and peace. The eyes of the woman are
like (but the poet does not make this comparison) or
are the bright symbols and signs of blasonry. Thus

---

[22]Louÿs, Oeuvres, I, op. cit., pp. 188-189.

1 In your eyeballs transparent like a
rainbow, Matutinal disappears
The tornado of the night senses
The swarm of the hardly bridled beasts

2 Red chimeras which weave
On the stems under the corollas
Fantastic Will-o'-the-wisps
in bar on the profound sky;

3 Golden Griffons with black wings
Spread in flight on the shield
Among the lilies where have lived
Only in the dream as possible flowers

4 Green and silvery fish
Hatched as torsos of mermaids
Unicorns tripping under the reins
And, head to the ground, charging;

the images of strophes 2,3,4,5, and 6 work in both
directions, toward the woman as arouser and appeaser
of passion. The image of the woman as arousing
passion is already in strophe 1 ("L'essaim des bêtes
mal bridées") brought into contact with the eiry images
of the heart of the poem, and the dreamed weird de-
signs on the coat-of-arms work back toward the woman
("Griffons d'or...Parmi les lys ayant vécu/Dans le
seul songe efflorissable;"). What is more the heraldic
image is adjusted to the needs of the image of the
woman. The sensuous dream was a battle with wicked,
perverse, fantom-like night creatures of the imagina-
tion, monsters which are at one and the same time the
decorations of the shield and the monsters of passionate
sin which were likewise in the woman and in the dream
(indicating an interior conflict). The "Chimères de

5 Vampires whose dry feet get entrapped
in Some Nepenthe and water lilies
Everything vanishes like a curtain
On a virgin limpidity

6 And, sins of dawn with unwholesome eyes,
Fever of livid circles around eyes
Dangerous form of avid bodies
Which a wind suspends at the cape of
breasts

7 Double dream which is divided into
four quarters of purple with the gold
of the blason, The fuliginous fleece
Stumbling on the immortal clasping,

8 They all are assuaged. But the strange
Psychical flight extends its illimitable
span in which is transfigured A flight
of pictures on a golden ground

9 And dawn makes flourish ideas as
The whirlwind of the senses from the
night which becomes smooth and unfolds
in your pupils, transparent like a
rainbow.

gueules," the "Griffons d'or aux ailes de sable," and
the "Poissons de sinople et d'argent"are a part of the
coat-of-arms: Gueules evokes the heraldic color, red,
and the same applies for sable, black, argent, silver,
and sinople, green. This poem is a motif of conquest
of passion by tranquillity where the terms are primarily geared toward an erotic meaning. Its particular value is found in the stress placed on the sub-
conscious. Human beings, like coat-of-arm figures
are enigmatic and controlled in the morning (the
conscious level of activity). Then their directed
actions, their watched looks, their arranged appearance
do not any longer betray hidden conflicts underneath.
It is only in the darkness of night that inhibitions
are lost in the privacy of chambers. Better still
and coinciding with the imagery of the poem, it is
only in the dream-filled hours of sleep that the unconscious unchains the horde of repressed desires and
hostilities, which act to their fullness on the hidden
and macabre battlefield of the unconscious. As has
been remarked by Louÿs' editor, the last strophe's
idées, iridées, is more than a faint echo of Mallarmé's
"Prose pour des Esseintes."

André Fontainas has continued the Symbolist
tradition of poetry conceived as its own subject. His
"Danseuse" is a motif development on poetic inspiration and creation. The conquest to be achieved is
the pure poem:

Nul fleuve, si ce n'est pas la flamme à des bras
Bercé, n'ondule encore en étreintes lascives:
Je vois tout le sourire au soleil de ces rives
Mûrir le vain trésor dont tu te souviendras.

Va. Le flux se propage aux parfums de pétales
Dans l'air que trouble à peine une ride, ô jardin
Des horizons evanescents et purs soudain
Sous l'immobile nuit des étoiles natales.

Mais un appel révèle au rêve son émoi
De suivre une aile brusque aux porches du silence
Flamboyer, puis s'éteindre, éclairs! d'où ne s'élance
L'essaim nouveau vers l'ombre de vivre, ou vers moi;

Et pour l'astre, seul beau, que du pied tu désignes
Se dévêt l'ardent vol, ô Danseuse! des cygnes. 23

When we think of Mallarmé's prose on the Ballet, Fontainas' choice of the dancer as a symbol of poetic
creation becomes significant. The sonnet is a rhapsody
of the dance, a sketching of the dancer's movements,
from first the arm movements to the fuller movements
of the legs, until they become so complete that the
ideal dance is born. It is necessary to think not of
the formalized classic ballet, but of modern dance as
initiated by Isadora Duncan, dance at a moment when
it is a spontaneous and actual creation. Thus the

---

[23]Fontainas, _Choix_, pp. 56-57.

No river, except perhaps the flame with arms
Cradled, still undulates in lascivious embraces:
I see all the smiling under the sun of these shores
Ripen the vain treasure which you will remember

Go. the movement spreads with the perfumes of the petals
In the air which scarcely a ripple troubles, o garden
From the horizons disappearing and suddenly pure
Under the still night of stars appearing

But a call reveals its emotion to the dream
To follow a quick wing to porches of silence,
Blazes, then extinguished, Lightning ! from which is
not launched a new swarm toward the shadow of living
or toward me;

And for the star, alone beautiful, that you trace
with your foot/is divested the ardent flight, O
Dancer! of the swans.

dancer may at first commence with normal, almost
manneristic movements which vaguely recall past
accomplishments, and hint at the possibilities of the
future. Here the movements may seem like a river or
a flame beyond which can be seen the shores of the
ideal creation. Initially, however, the dancer, like
the jazz musician, is fumbling, the melody wanders in
and out of minor keys constantly searching for the
solution to the riddle. All movements here are in
flux, evanescent, ondulatory. Suddenly, however, the
dancer (and the musician) becomes transformed, the indistinguishable movements ("Des horizons evanescents")
are a purity of comprehension; the form becomes sure
and the movements are transformed. The dancer, hidden under the dance, becomes a "long metaphor." In
her movements she resumes all movement and enters into
the quiet realm of immobility. She is transformed
into a swan, as in Anna Pavlova's creations, and in
the fine movements of Valéry's Athikté.

The images applied to the dancer are intended
to apply to any art in its search for a pure form.
The poet has an interior disturbance because of his
need to create. His first essays are elusive and he
is not able to find the means to express the ideal.
In the dark night of creation, however, in an intuitive flash, the poet is able to perceive the ideal
which carries him into a realm bordering on silence.
The ideal is there ("Flamboyer") only not to be
there ("s'éteindre"). As the dancer traces a star
with her feet, the poet finds the inspired words which
create the swan. Three steps are discernible then in
the poem: ondulation, precision, and achievement. This
is an excellent motif of the poetic conquest. The
modern dancer is the ideal symbol of movement and
sound in its search for form, in the act of becoming.
Consequently, the actual physical expression of what
is an abstract act, especially for poetry, is more
than adequately evoked, and saved from inferior
discursive or allegorical expression.

Conquest with a predominant emphasis on poetic conquest is the subject of Pierre Louÿs' "Les Aigles" with which we shall conclude our discussion of this motif:

Le burg monstrueux d'ombre et les tours surplombantes
Usurpateurs de l'épouvantement des vents
Ecoutent dans l'effroi des ténèbres tombantes
Les Héros fils de Dzeus et les dieux survivants
Conquérir la montagne aux cris des corybantes.

Venus des eaux, des bois, des prés bleus, des étangs,
Des brises, descendus des cieux, montés des vagues,
Ils marchent à l'assaut des hautes portes vagues
De la Nuit Romantique et du Songe et des Temps.

Ils marchent, éblouis, couverts de lumière, ivres
De fondre à leur soleil les neiges et les givres
Et d'enfoncer le jour dans le mur crevassé;

Et voici qu'au-dessus des armes et des torches,
Beaux, et foudroyant d'or le noir deuil du Passé, [24]
Les aigles blancs passent à travers les grands porches

The central image is of a conquering army storming a mountain castle which they are about to keep for good. Three levels of meaning can be seen in the image. First the poem appears as an evocation of a victorious army about to claim a mountain top fortress. The city is

---

[24]Louÿs, Oeuvres, I, op. cit., p. 57.

The monstrous dark burg and the overhanging towers
Usurpers of the terror of the winds
Hear in the fright of the falling shadows
The Heros sons of Zeus and the surviving gods
Conquering the mountain to the cries of the corybantes.

covered with shadows; in some ways it is like a mon-
ster about to be destroyed. In a dark and terrifying
night it awaits the arrival of the young and powerful
army. More likely, however, the conquerors represent
modern man who again desires to be god-like. The
conquerors are survivors of a heavenly realm, the displaced children of Olympus who desire to reconquer
the mountain top from which they have been exiled.
Specifically and with echoes of the whole nineteenth
century poetic tradition, the conquerors are the poets
challenging the mountain of sterility which keeps
them earthbound. Conquest of the mountain is the
conquest of poetry ("De la Nuit Romantique et du
Songe et des Temps"). The first tercet, with a tinge
of allegory, makes it clearer still that the conquest
is a poetic one. The poets covered with light, drunk
with the practice of their ritual ("...aux cris des
corybantes") march forward melting the snow and frost

Coming from the waters, woods, blue meadows, ponds,
From the breezes, coming down from the heavens,
coming up from the waves, They march to the assault
of the high vague gates of the Romantic Night, of the
Dream, and of Times.

They march, dazzled, covered by light, drunk
To melt at their sun the snows and the frost
And to thrust the day into the split wall;

And here above the arms and the torches
Handsome, and blasting with gold, the black wake
of the Past/The white eagles pass through the large
portals.

(sterility), break down the walls of the city, open
blocked walls to light. In the final strophe they
have conquered the mountain and achieved the poetic
realm. Light conquering darkness, whatever this may
symbolize, is the theme of the poem.

The poems of conquest which we have just analyzed vary in quality, some bordering on a personal
lyricism, while others soar into a realm of symbolic
abstraction. In all cases there is at least a veil-
ing, and a sublimation of the lyric to the supra-lyric.
The Tristan poem of De Régnier and "En vos prunelles"
of Louÿs are constantly in danger of a particular
and erotic lyricism. This does not happen, however,
because the imagery is capable of greater intricacies
of meaning. The same can be said of Louÿs' "Le burg
monstrueux" and of Fontainas' "Danseuse" where an
allegorical penchant is barely avoided. We have tried
to make it clear in the explications that regardless
of how dominant one aspect of an evocation may be,
other interpretations are not precluded. In the
final analysis this must be the test for all motif
symbol poems. De Régnier's "Au Sommet de la proue"
is the purest motif of conquest we have found. As
we have shown in our analysis, no single element
dominates to the exclusion of another. The symbol
contains a great number of ambiguous interpretations,
all of which are valid.

Motif of Disillusion and Hope

A final category of motifs remains to be
examined, that of disillusionment and hope, fundamental conditions of humankind which can be observed in
the poetry of the minor Symbolists. This motif com-
plements the previous three, and all four can truly
be said to express the four-faced personality of man:
man alone in the world, the need of men for fulfillment,
man the dominator and possessor, and man with his broken heart and dreams.

The motif of disillusion is the poetic expression
of a basic human paradox. Art has always been aware of
this peculiarity of man by which he heroically struggles
to attain a desired object only to lose interest once
it seems possessed. The search for the dream seems
more important than the possession. As society progressively goes through a process of de-spiritualization,
man seeks completion where it can be found least, namely
in a sensuality, and consequently arrives more quickly
at despair.

A new spiritualism centering in hope combats
this condition. In some cases it is the revival of
religious beliefs, in others the making the best of
an existing situation, in still others a secular and
humanistic faith in tomorrow.

Such is the situation as it is found in the
poetry of the minor Symbolists, and the poems of this
section will illustrate some aspects of it. For the
reasons just given we have collected these poems under
the double standard of disillusion and hope. The despair at the end of the nineteenth century seldom reaches
the razor's edge condition of mid-twentieth century
Existentialism. In each of the poems examined the black
night is accompanied by the hope for a brighter morning.

Again we commence our inquiry with Henri de
Régnier whose sonnet "Nous voguions sur des mer de nuit"
is a motif of mutual happiness in a love transcending
the hardships of life:

Nous voguions sur des mer de nuit et de colères,
Loin de la Terre et de l'Eternelle Saison
Où l'or de tes cheveux fut la seule moisson,
Loin des Jardins fleuris et des Jouvenes claires;

L'évanouissement de rives et de choses
Douces et mortes et plus lointaines toujours
Nous fit pleurer tous deux, et des arômes lourds
Parfumaient notre exil de mémoires de roses;

L'enfantin Paradis qu'un caprice dévaste,
Du mauvais sortilège et de l'ombre néfaste,
Filet mystérieux où trébucha ma foi,

Surgit comme au lever des aurores premières,
Et revoici, telles qu'alors, toutes pour Toi,
Guirlande à la fontaine et torsades trémières![25]

The motif is centered around the image of a voyage
(which transcends allegory because of the imprecise
terms) from a land or situation where a woman was entirely filling the life of the man. The motif is
effected through the constant appearance of the image
of the original happiness which vacillates between existence and non-existence.

     The first strophe opens with a visualization
of the exile of the two lovers from a garden of Eden.
Where there was happiness there is now only night and
disharmony. The realization of the loss is apparent
in the second and third strophes. In the fourth strophe
the paradise is regained by sheer loving remembrance.

[25]De Régnier, _Premiers Poèmes_, p. 236.

We were sailing on the seas of night and wrath
Far from Land and the Eternal Season
Where the gold of your hair was the only harvest
Far from the flowering gardens and bright Youth;

The disappearance of the shores and of things
Sweet and dead and always more distant
Made both of us cry, and heavy aromas
Perfumed our exil with memories of roses;

The children's Paradise which a caprice devastates
Some evil magic and some unlucky shadow
Mysterious thread on which my faith stumbled,

Rises up like at daybreak of first dawns
And here they are again, all for You like in earlier
times/The Garland at the fountain and the twisted
hollyhocks!

This situation is evoked by the image of the
voyage. At first an image is created of the two lovers
on the high seas in exile from their native land. In
the second strophe we receive the impression that their
boat is still within sight of land, for they are just
far enought out at sea for the shore line to become
indistinguishable from the horizon ("L'évanouissement
de rêves et de choses"). Only the perfume of the
flowers such as would be found on a tropical island,
thus preserved strongest in their memories, floats
across the waves ("...et des aromes lourds/Parfumaient
notre exil de mémoires de roses;") and joins the lovers
to their lost paradise which is to be a paradise psycho-
logically and gradually regained. It lingers as bliss
in the hair of the beloved woman. The first tercet
implies that it was by magic, by some sort of deception
("Du mauvais sortilège et de l'ombre néfaste") that the
paradise was lost, most probably by a fundamental mis-
understanding. Hope is introduced in the second tercet.
The ship carries the lovers away from their kingdom
but restores, in their loneliness, the original harmony.
This would be entirely consistent with our explanation
of the poem.

The voyage image in space may also work as a
voyage through time. The original happiness of youth
is lost across the years. Disillusionment takes place
followed by realization and a hopeful and successful
effort to regain a part of the happiness of youth,
especially through the happy memories and a forgetting
of the bad ones. The poem as it would apply to the
man and his wife could explained as follows: The
young couple,after the first honeymoon, went into the
hardships of life. The man busy with affairs of the
world finds that the woman partner is not the only thing
in life. There are hardships stronger than love, and
without realization, the original fervor of love is
lost in the matter of fact occupations of daily life.
In their middle years both have strong feelings of
solitude, and souvenirs of the past cannot dispel their
present sorrow. Suddenly, however, with even greater

age, the childlike paradise of yore, transformed, once
again becomes clear. They both feel as if the first
dawn of their love had reappeared. Freed from the an-
xieties of life the woman becomes essential again for
life, and the man contemplates in tranquillity the landscape and dreams of youth.

This sonnet is a particularly happy motif poem
which corresponds exactly to the actuality of the husband and wife relationship. Claudel will treat the same
subject with a different resolution in his Cantate à
trois voix. Here the solution is in the tradition of
Verhaeren's poems to his wife. The initial collapse of
of the young dream of love causing disillusion is replaced in the autumn years of life by a mellowed return
to the first love. Where this is accomplished it is
done so by the actual separation itself. The years of
disillusion provoke inquiry into the real situation,
provide an acceptance of limitations, and make the original love return with a greater understanding and spiritual intensity.

"Hommage à Victor Hugo" of Pierre Louÿs offers
a variation of the pattern of disillusion and hope, and
can be called a motif of transformation:

Le Satyre, Amour roux qu'il créa dieu des dieux,
L'a repris pour soi-même et le porte à la tombe
Cadavre, mains d'où la clarté gouttèle et tombe
Et qui livrent la lyre au vent mélodieux.

Il creusera la fosse à l'ombre d'un vieux arbre
Près d'une source, où les nymphes d'eau souriront.
Le soir, l'une viendra s'y défleurir le front,
Et, tendre pour le Mort, couronnera son marbre.

Alors, penchant les mains sur les joncs palpitants,
Pan verra luire au ciel merveilleux des étangs
Un pays pur de lune et de laiteux mystère

Et la nuit sous les bois est de si triste argent
Qu'il pensera rêver tout au coeur de la terre
L'âme, parmi des prés d'asphodèles, songeant.[26]

The Satyr, the rough violator of the wood nymphs is
completely dissatisfied with the rough love he has always pursued. Nay this too burning love actually des-
troys him and buries him in the woods near a source.
In the evening one of the nymphs whom he used to pursue,
comes to the grave, and out of a sentiment of pity and
love for her former enemy, now transformed, she puts
some flowers from her wreath on his tomb, a symbolic
expression of love for the dead Satyr. Pan, the god
of the nymphs, is astonished by the signs of peace
which effect a change in the erstwhile amorous landscape of the forest. Now there is a pure landscape of
moonlight, and the woods are silvery. The soul of the

---

[26]Louÿs, Oeuvres, I, op. cit., p. 81.

The Satyr, Red Love which he made god of the gods
Retook him for itself and carries him to the tomb
A cadaver, hands from which the brightness drops and
Falls, and which give up the lyre to the melodious wind.

He will dig the hole in the shade of an old tree
Near a spring where the water nymphs will smile.
In the evening, one will come to take flowers from
her forehead, and, affectionate toward the dead one,
will crown his tomb.

Then, leaning his hands on the quivering rushes
Pan will see glistening in the marvelous sky of
the ponds, a pure country with moon and lacteous
mystery

Satyr, purified by the sacrifice of the water nymph,
dreams of bliss as found in the fields of daffodils.
    This poem evokes a spiritualization of love.
A Satyr, like the one of Mallarmé, is converted to a
new type of love through death. The same red hot love
which made him a Satyr kills and buries him in order
to make something better of him. The nymph placing
flowers on the tomb symbolizes the acknowledgment of
the transformation of the Satyr. This echoes the legend
of Beauty and the Beast, for the nymph is able to re-
cognize beauty in ugliness, even virtue where there was
impurity, the possibilities (here post-mortem) of a
spiritualization. As water, source, and nymph mean
the same thing, the water refreshes and irrigates the
rough ground in which the Satyr is buried, and it is
as though the dead Satyr felt that his grave is transformed into a field of daffodils.
    Disillusionment in love followed by hope and
transformation of the love is the subject of Ghil's
"Pour L'Enfant ancienne" where the poet interprets
the meaning of the vicissitudes of a past love, hence
the title:

Tue en l'étonnement de nos yeux mutuels
Qui délivrèrent là l'or de latentes gloires,
Que, veuve dans le Temple aux signes rituels,
L'onde d'éternité réprouve nos mémoires.

And the night under the woods is of so sad a silver
That he (Pan) will think the soul (of the Satyr)
is dreaming in the very heart of the earth, as
though it were among the fields of asphodels.

118

Tel instant qui naissait des heurts éventuels
Tout palmes de doigts longs aux nuits ondulatoires
Vrais en le dôme espoir des vols perpétuels
Nous ouvrit les passés de nos pures histoires

Une moire de vains soupirs pleure sous les
Trop seuls saluts riants par nos voeux exhalés,
Aussi haut qu'un néant de plumes vers les gnoses.

Advenus rêves des vitraux pleins de demains
Doux et nuls à pleurer, et d'un midi de roses,
Nous venons l'un à l'autre en élevant les mains.[27]

When they first met the lovers thought that their mutual
possession was everything needed for happiness. In
the mutual surprise of their love the past experiences
of humanity, seen as a roaring wave, went unheard ("Tue
en l'étonnement de nos yeux mutuels"). Their love
brought forth joy and the best qualities ("...l'or de
latentes gloires") of each. The eternal love rites,

---

[27]Ghil, in Van Bever and Léautaud, op. cit.,
I, p. 99.

Silenced in the admiration of our mutual eyes
Which set free there the gold of latent glories,
Like a widow in the Temple with ritual signs,
The wave of eternity disapproves our recollections

Such a moment which was born of possible clashes
All long-fingered hands in the undulating nights
True in the dome hopes of perpetual flights
Opened for us the past of our pure histories.

A moire of vain sighs cries under the
Too isolated laughing salvations exhaled by our vows,
As high as a nothingness of flights toward the Gnoses

Befallen dreams of stained glass windows full of tomorrows
Sweet and incapable to cry, and of a noonday of roses,
We come to each other raising our hands.

however, brought doubts, the love partner was not always equal to the dream, and there were signs of de-
terioration and a possible ending of the love ("Que,
veuve dans le Temple aux signes rituels"). The love
was not always serene ("aux nuits ondulatoires"), and
their hope of perpetually soaring ("Vrais en le dôme
espoir des vols perpétuels") into an ideal realm became a flight into the "néant." The destruction of
the ideal brought bitter disillusionment. It taught
the lovers, however, a higher type of love. Hence the
flight of love was transformed into a desperate, power-
less quest for spiritual love and truth ("...un néant
de plumes vers les gnoses"). But the dream of love,
a spiritual love, was clearly brought home by the
story of saints as pictured on stained glass windows.
The young lovers then marched together toward a spiritual future with hands no longer joined in embrace, or
struggle, but hands uplifted in prayer. This sonnet
is a motif of mutual relations not to be fulfilled,
accompanied by disillusion and transformation of the
love into a spiritual quest.

Louÿs' "Sonnet pour un éventail" is a motif
of illusion centering in the idea of dream and poetic
creation:

> D'une main si triste mouvante
> Où chatoie un éventail noir
> Avec ces plumes au miroir
> Une invisible Eve s'évente.
>
> Les yeux mi-fermés elle invente
> Un cygne sur un lac du soir
> Elle sent monter et déchoir
> Une aile en silence rêvante
>
> D'où s'effile vers ce tableau
> Légère d'ombres et de rêve
> Une fin de plumes sur l'eau

> Où l'ombre invisible d'une Eve
> Qui d'un grand geste épanouit
> Le vaste éventail de la nuit.[28]

Louÿs' editor has remarked on the influence of Mallarmé
in this poem: "Influence très nette de Mallarmé (Sainte);
...préfiguration de Valéry."[29]

A woman stands before a mirror, her face half-
hidden by a fan. A vain woman with eyes half-closed,
she playfully imagines that she is a black swan. In
the first tercet the woman has been transformed into a
black swan which is dying on the waters, and night comes
(second tercet) and the blackness of the swan is swallowed
up in the darkness of the night. The poem thus involves
the néant, alludes to the original disillusionment, Eve
and the loss of Paradise, plus numerous implications of
the night for the woman (humanity) and the poet.

---

[28] Louÿs, Oeuvres, I, op. cit., p. 78.

[29] Ibid., p. 335.

> With a hand so sadly moving
> In which glistens a black fan
> With these feathers at a mirror
> An invisible Eva fans herself.
>
> With eyes half-closed she imagines
> A swan on a lake at dusk
> She feels ascending and falling
> A wing dreaming in silence
>
> From which comes out toward this picture
> Light like in shadows and dream
> A close of wings on the water
>
> Where the invisible shadow of an Eva
> Who with a great movement opens
> The Vast fan of the night.

The woman before the mirror does something playful, as perhaps the poet might do in the writing of a
poem. Out of a playful, seemingly innocent act come
grave implications. The woman and the poet get some in-
sight into their vanity. They both half-seriously create
the image of a black swan, and are suddenly overwhelmed
by the significance of their own creation. There is a
hint to an explanation that the black swan is the néant
which covers them and causes despair. From a playful
act comes the constant destruction of mankind through
"Night" and through Eve.

The motif of disillusion and hope is closest
to Mallarmé in Jean Royère's "La caresse du soir sur
ce marbre fantôme":

> La caresse du soir sur ce marbre fantôme,
> Atome inhabité frôlant d'autres atomes,
> Neige, pour une nuque ironique à souhait,
> Dans le nonchaloir que le crépuscule fait
> Peser sur le ciel gris qui de l'azur se gare
> Et tourne au noir ! C'est la mélancolique gare
> Où s'embarque au déclin de l'arrière-clarté,
> Le soir espoir humain veuf de son entité. [30]

Here the image is most elusive. The poem achieves its
effect in the epic symbolization of static objects which

---

[30] Royère, Poésies, p. 19.

The caress of the evening on this fantom marble
Uninhabited atom grazing other atoms
Snows, for an ironic nape as one would have it,
In the nonchalance that the twilight causes
To weigh on the gray sky which keeps some blue only
And turns to black ! It is the melancholy station
Where embarks at the decline of the last light
The evening human hope widow of its entity.

resume many lyric possibilities. At first it appears
that the evening light is cast upon a statue, and
illuminates its neck. This is done in the hazard of
the twilight forcing itself upon the gray sky, which
is trying to become night. The statue which in the
daytime seems clear and alives, becomes in the darkness
like the widow of human hope who is about to depart on
the night train.

A better interpretation would force us to concentrate not on a statue image, but on a living woman
expected to sit down at a marble mantle of a fireplace.
From here the thought jumps to the station image which
is central to the poem. The motif splashes out on a
white station in the twilight, where the gray of the
sky is stronger than the slight remainders of blue. In
the station is the human personality grieving over what
he or she has lost, but nevertheless filled with some
new hope. This could be a fresh young widow or widower
who is leaving a place of sad memories to try a new life
in a distant place, or a dying person drawing close to
death, filled with melancholy, but yet hopeful for a
better life beyond the grave. Even the white marble
station is hope, and the glimmer of daytime in the twilight of evening. Despair and hope are reiterated
through the constant opposition and fusion of light and
dark, producing multiple images of hope and despair.

Like the other categories we have established,
these motifs vary in artistic value. More than the
other categories the point of departure is more often
found in a human and lyric situation which has always
been poetically expressed, and which becomes part of
the motif expression. This is very evident in the De
Régnier poem with which we started our discussion. The
implications are obvious. Disillusionment followed by
hope is a common lyric situation. It is more apt to
have obvious manifestations in life situations than the
more subtle subjects of conquest and incompletion which
come to have an almost new imagery in modern poetry.
Further it is a reduction of tension and the loss of
frustration. Disillusionment and hope enter into not

only the more profound human situations of love, ideal,
death, but also find manifestations in the more banal
aspects of life. For these reasons they are more likely
to undergo a lyric rather than a motif expression. Significantly, hope is an element which is excluded from
the work of Mallarmé, unless we take the unresigned
resignation and angoisse of the swan as a type of hope,
which is highly improbable. There is a backward gradation then from Mallarmé, without hope, the wavering
of the semi-Symbolist Valéry, "...il faut tenter de
vivre!", the lyric-motif expression of the minor Symbolist poets, to the full Romantic effusion.
    We have considered all of the poems in this
section as motifs of disillusion and hope. Only one,
however, the poem of Royère, is a pure motif, and in
this he has given Mallarméan expression to a sentiment
obviously missing from the work of the master.
    The analysis in which we have been engaged
demonstrates how the image becomes a symbol under the
direction of the motif. With few exceptions is it
possible to limit the image to the realm of the particular object as in lyric poetry. Symbolism in fact
means a reversal of the lyric order. Whereas lyric
poetry pivots on the particular, absence from the
native habitat, the loss of a loved one, ennui, idealism,
the motif symbol poem grasps for the universal, the
idea behind the image. The image is seized in its
universal condition where it has lost its accidental
properties, and is on the point of disappearing. When
the image is so created, all the multiple aspects of
the particular are able to emanate from the essence.
Motif Symbolism then may be seen as an ultimate refinement of the theory of correspondance of Baudelaire. The
artist continues to imitate nature, but with a new
vision which precludes the accidental and makes for the
evocation of a pure and impervious beauty. Mallarmé
is largely responsible for such an actuality.

The poems we have quoted are not comparable to the perfect gems of Mallarmé. This results from the fact that these poets are minor and inferior craftsmen, plus the fact that their sensibilities require a different expression. Imperfect as these examples may be, they are indicative of the actual influence of Mallarmé on the minor Symbolist poets.

Hermetic structure as initiated by Mallarmé does not necessarily mean that poetry is bent on the motif. For this reason, we shall discuss for some pages the intellectual, manneristic, hermetic poetry which is a major aspect of minor Symbolist production.

When Svend Johansen insists on the primacy of image over thought, he makes the essential distinction necessary in the evaluation of Symbolist poetry. Our research has been carried out under the guidance of this principle, and on the basis of it we evaluated the poems under study. Our study would not be complete, however, without an appraisal of the hermetic poems of the minor poets where thought precedes image, where a veiled allegory and an obscure description are hidden in a hermetic structure, where hermetic poetry and poésie pure appear definitely confused. The symbolic poems we have studied are unfortunately a small part of the entire work of the minor poets. In most cases, as with Valéry, a hermetic allegorism or a manneristic description is the result where a symbolism is intended. Thus the lyricism we noted in Chapter II continues in the modern poetic form. Hermetic poetry neither guarantees originality nor Symbolism.

The examples of allegory are not as numerous as the descriptive poems. Allegories continue to be written on traditional subjects, within the new form, and there is a tendency to create allegories on the poetic creation as such.

Jean Royère's "Allégresse ! c'est les matins"
is an allegory expressing the poet's determined desire
to find joy against the forces of fate. The poem
illustrates a hermetic personfication and image dispersion. Happiness is personified in the arrival of
dawn who is without the cares and worries of life,
work, and scholarship ("...pieds des dimanches,"
"...treize ans philistins," "...De jaunes rayons lib-
ertins"). Three more images are utilized to complete
the picture: a sparrow glutted with food screeches and
dies, life becomes a creature waddling down a sidewalk,
and the poet digs up the cadaver of Yorrick. These
images are intellectual equations. They mean that
life is a gamble, man has no control over his fate,
and therefore it is better to take whatever happiness
is offered and register no complaint.

> Allégresse ! c'est les matins
> Venus sur leurs pieds des dimanches
> Avec leurs treize ans philistins
> Dans la chambre où six heures penchent
> Sur la veilleuse qui s'éteint
> De jaunes rayons libertins
> Glissés entre les joints des planches !
> Le moineau piaille qui demain
> Ira pourrir sous les pervenches
> Trop gavé d'eau tiède et de pain,
> Jusqu'au jour où, miroir sans tain
> De ce présent qui se déhanche
> Sur les trottoirs de mon destin,
> J'allais déterrer le mutin
> Petit cadavre yorrick teint
> D'une odeur de sève et de branches.[31]

The same note is present in Fontainas' "Le
Satyre." The action of the allegory is obscured until
the poet offers an explanation and philosophical comment

---

[31]Ibid., p. 50.

in the last strophe. A satyr pursues a nymph whom he
desires. He ravages her, and is stunned to discover
that he has killed her. The poet explains the meaning:
all happiness is ephemeral, nothing last.

Cueille, Satyre, un rire à des griffes de roses.
L'héroïque parfum exalte de sa joie
Le dédain empourpré des corolles écloses.

C'est midi. L'ombre bleue aux grands ormes s'éploie,
Le fleuve lourd s'entasse autour des feuilles lentes
D'où ton oeil d'or épie en des frissons ta proie.

Tout le rêve, un baiser dont fou tu l'ensanglantes,
S'ouvre à des vols soudains d'élytres vers l'azur
Sur qui tu clos l'essor des paumes ruisselantes.

La nymphe est morte. Les nymphes! Le sort est dur.
Ecoute: que ta vie, éprise de mensonge,
S'éjouisse à dormir au pied de quelque mur;

Qu'importe? le bonheur de la vie est un songe.[32]

     Mallarmé is the subject of testimonial allegories
by Fontainas and Louÿs. These allegories are inter-
esting because of the effort to honor the poet by an
imitation of his own poems. The second sonnet of
Fontainas' group of poems on Valvins, the summer home
of Mallarmé, expresses the gratitude of the poet to
Mallarmé for the work he has accomplished, the vistas
he has opened. The countryside of Valvins is described
as a "Prose pour des Esseintes" land where the kiss of
the flowers by the sylvains turns them into butterflies.
Mallarmé is personified as Valvins, as a guiding star,
and finally in the last strophe he appears as a Captain
of the ship of poetry.

L'eau plus lente s'écoule autour des touffes frêles
Et, naïve, elle vire et s'étire, ô jeux vains,
Jusqu'aux portes d'un rêve où se rient les sylvains
A suivre frais baisers, naître aux tiges, leurs ailes.

[32] Fontainas, Choix, p. 27.

L'arome astral d'or mûr en cent tourelles
Au fleuve, et filtre aux fleurs ivres de tous les vins:
C'est, où vivre parmi les hêtres clairs, Valvins,
Et l'argent de leurs troncs s'allonge en reflets grêles.

La rive s'humilie en prairie et s'étend
Proche l'azur et brûle au soleil palpitant,
Millier extasié d'herbe où vibre une étoile;

Mais la proue a mordu vers l'arche un fluvial
Remous, et s'éparpille en frisson lilial
Tout l'air léger et net, qu'illumine la Voile.[33]

        "Rade aux frissons futurs" of Fontainas also
appears to be a very difficult poem, but close examination reveals a construction so discursive that the
whole poem may be restated in prose terms with few
difficulties. The poet addresses the people of a
small, innocent, tropical paradise, and tells them to
fear storms because they will drive ships in peril to
land, and the people will be corrupted by the strangers.
The island is described as a lovely garden spot, free
of corruption (black clouds, storms, impure cups). The
second quatrain shows how the poet obscures the description. This is accomplished by a mixing up of the terms,
the subject repeats under different persons, the verb
is put in a minimal position, and it becomes difficult
to find the correct object for each subject. The nouns
are thus given prominent relief, the image gains ascendancy, but thought remains primary: the city with
joy and in triumph decorates the littoral to welcome
the ships, while the priests, without any great display,
refuse to take part in the activities:

---

        [33]Ibid., pp. 51-52. See also Louÿs, Oeuvres,
I, p. 75.

Rade aux frissons futurs des océans d'aurores,
Sera-ce en le reflet d'un lointain vespéral
Que des vaisseaux cimés de leur azur astral
Attérriront aux quais de tes jardins sonores?

Ville, ô Toi, du triomphe et de fleurs, qui décores
De joie, avec ta foule en fête, un littoral
Où des prêtres sans pompe et sans deuil augural
Se détournent de boire en d'impures amphores:

Garde l'orgueil de vivre et l'orgueil dans l'amour
Et la douceur frémissante d'un songe chaste,
Orgueil candide, aux yeux vers la mer, sur la tour,

Vigile, des mâts d'ombre errent par la mer vaste;
Vent du large, menace sombre aux jardins clairs,
Crains le nuage gros de tempête et d'éclairs.[34]

The ratio between a real symbolistic motif poem and a
mannered-hermetic one is almost the same as that between
an impressionistic and a pointillistic picture. Although
the pointillistic picture at first sight appears almost
as a refinement of the impressionistic one, at close
inspection it reveals itself as a geometrical construct
only, not born out of artistic necessity.

Henri de Régnier's most hermetic poem, "Nul
ne sait si promis" is a mannered poem which contains
none of the motif symbol possibilities of some of his
less obscure poems. The chief value to be obtained in
this poem, as is the case with so many of the poems of
Góngora, is to make a beautiful construction out of a
situation which is primarily descriptive and static.
Musing upon the thought of a person of royal blood
exiled to a desert island, the poet expresses the pro-
blemless situation in a manner which obscures thought,
but which can be solved like a puzzle. In the first
strophe, the poet thinks about the reason for the exile.
It is quite possible, but impossible to know for a fact,
that a star shining over the bed of the royal hero
when he was a child, announced the exile of the future.

---

34 Ibid., p. 23.

The star was not seen, however, its warning could not
be heeded, and the prophecy came true. The second
quatrain describes the hero walking on the beach, and
explains the color of seashells. The young man picks
up a seashell, blows into it, and the contact with his
lips (the royal personage as a creator figure) gives
it the richness of his voice, and the pink color of his
lips. In the first tercet he is described as surrounded
by a swarm of bees in flight, and walking over the sands
he steps on hidden treasures. To subsist, he kills
birds with a bow and arrow, and when he bathes, dawn
blushes in embarrassment at his royal nakedness. The
hero is the mannered device by which De Régnier draws
an indirect nature picture:

> Nul ne sait si promis à quelque exil farouche,
> Héros maudit de son règne déshérité,
> D'astre annonciateur d'une nativité
> N'a pas brillé jadis sa puérile couche;
>
> Et la conque où s'éveille aux gammes de sa bouche
> Le progressif écho d'une sonorité
> Garde au contact de son pur souffle ébruité
> Un peu du rose de la lèvre qui la touche.
>
> Il rayonne à son front des vols d'abeilles d'ors.
> Au poids de son talon résonnent des trésors
> Enfouis en l'horreur de cette solitude
>
> Où sa flèche tua les Oiseaux voyageurs,
> Et quand sa vierge chair pour le bain se dénude
> L'aube d'un sang royal y montre ses rougeurs. [35]

Jean Royère has many descriptive poems, the
majority of them being love lyrics. "Moins l'azur
dans le flot" describes how an older poet fell in love

---

[35] De Régnier, _Premiers Poèmes_, p. 178.

130

with a girl much younger than he. The poem opens with
a lyric comparison, the union of the blue waves of the
ocean was no greater than the love he had for this
young girl (lines 1,2). Because of the difference in
their age, he used to meet her on the seashore, where
the proper people of the town could not spy on them,
and laugh at them (lines 3,4). This was a romantic
affair because the girl and he understood each other
better than the harmonious sea understood its own
union. She received his love ("...où ne me contrarie")
in spite of his older age ("lèvres fanées"). He
compares the girl to a "lis écarlate" because she was
pure, "lis", and stainless and gave herself to him
"écarlate." The poet concludes by comparing himself
to an old flower which had long ago lost its bloom,
but nevertheless enjoyed a brief summer of reflowering
with the young girl. The poet, however, older and
overwhelmed with sorrow and care, was not able to
continue the affair, for the time came when the girl
would have to seek a more suitable love partner. This
is a romantic poem of regret of a past love put into
a mannered setting which wantonly obscures the meaning.

> Moins l'azur dans le flot s'enchante et se marie
> Que mon rêve au votre s'incarne,
> Belle rive dormante, où ne me contrarie
> Quand l'oeil se colle à la lucarne
> Ni le regret d'aimer proche la berge amène
> La déesse rieuse aux contours indécis
> Que la brise indolente éparpille et ramène,
> Soeur du lis écarlate et du jaune souci,
> Ni de votre tiédeur me sentir engourdi,
> Laiteuse chair qui pâme à mes lèvres fanées
> Au refleurissement des roses surannées. 36

---

36 Royère, Poésies, p. 35.

We have not made any detailed analysis of these mannered poems, for we have only wanted to indicate their existence. In most cases, however, it would be impossible to extract much more meaning beyond what we have sketched here.

The evidence of an intellectual mannerism among the minor Symbolists has the following implications. It indicates that traditional lyric poetic themes were not effaced by the ascendancy of a hermetic and symbolic poetry. Hermetic poetry became the modern means of expression through Mallarmé. Many of the minor Symbolists, regardless of their own personal feelings, felt the obligation of their times to be "modern" without the sensibility that linked the new form to a new content. Thus they imitated poetic formulas for which they had no necessary content, a disharmony arose between the content and the form, and a mannerism was born. Such a clear cut situation cannot exist but theoretically, however, and may not be applied without reservations to the Symbolists as poets. In the cases of many of the poets we have quoted, they often achieved a veritable motif, while at other times they fell back into a mannerism. This is the second implication of the Symbolist manneristic poems, and is explained by the fact that the majority of Symbolists were enjoying a double ideal. Not pure Symbolists, not pure lyric poets, the contents and forms became a jungle of few consistent and discernible patterns. Lastly, a mannerism is produced by a pure policy of artful imitation without actual willing consent to, let alone understanding of the poetic ideal. In this last case, only Pierre Louÿs is capable of such an intellectual mannerism, and his motif symbol achievements seem to make even a pure mannerism debatable in his work. Like the other poets, he probably, at least for the extent of the Symbolist period, belongs in the second category mentioned.

Finally, an examination of pastiche-like imitations of Mallarmé would not be amiss, for the pastiche is not only evidence of a writer's influence, but by its overdoing of stylistic habits, through close imitation in a mannered sense, the artistic meaning of the pastiche throws light upon the original form.

Max Elskamp has written a very weak pastiche-like imitation of "Le Vierge, le vivace, et le bel aujourd'hui." This poem is of absolutely no value in understanding the original poem for Elskamp was incapable of imitating the whole cast of the original. Instead, he has taken the refrain pattern as a point of repair for his whole poem. It is very far from Mallarmé in spite of the analogical words such as "geai" to "cygne" which are only exterior imitations. We quote only two strophes:

> Mais geai qui paon se rêve aux plumes,
> Haut, ces tours sont-ce mes juchoirs?
> D'îles de Pâques aux fleurs noires
> Il me souvient en loins posthumes:
>
> Je suis un pauvre oiseau des îles.
>
> Or, d'avoir trop monté les hunes
> Et d'outre-ciel m'être vêtu,
> J'ai pris le mal des ingénus
> Comme une fièvre au clair de lune,
>
> Je suis un pauvre oiseau des îles.[37]

André Fontainas' "Rondels pour les musiciens" is a poor pastiche of "Surgi de la croupe et du bond." The form is changed from the sonnet to the rondeau. It is less a pastiche than an inept parody which not only uses "Surgi", but makes allusions to other poems such

---

[37]Elskamp, Louanges, pp. 89-90.

as "Hérodiade." Its only purpose is to amuse. It
is based on Mallarméan centos, and pays hommage to
Mallarmé by the use of whole locutions from his work:

> Surgi de la terre au zénith
> Parfums d'accords, rumeur et baume,
> Roulent les houles d'un grand psaume
> Tendre en sa force de granit.
>
> Il déferle, et, des l'introît,
> L'onde sonore emplit le dôme
> Surgi de la terre au zénith,
> Parfum d'accord, rumeur et baume,
>
> Quand, impérieux, Florent Schmitt
> Te dresse, désastre au royaume
> D'Hérode, Salome ! fantôme
> Eblouissant, au gré du rit
> Surgi de la terre au zénith.[38]

Fontainas' "La Voile" is a serious attempt at a pastiche
of "Une dentelle s'abolit," but it remains so far from
the original pattern, except for some tournures that
it is at the most only an acknowledgment that the real
Mallarmé is inimitable:

> Blancheur au ciel d'outremer
> Avant qu'un souffle l'efface,
> Une aile aigue émeut l'air,
> Glisse, s'éteint dans l'espace;
>
> Ton rêve fier d'un séjour
> Eployé selon la voile
> S'accroît quand s'exhale au jour
> Le frisson vif d'une étoile,

---

[38] Fontainas, Choix, p. 214.

> Et les vergers près des flots
> Tendent au bord qui rougeoie
> L'unique fruit de l'enclos
> Pour l'automne de ta joie [39]

Pierre Louÿs, as has been apparent throughout this study, was able to imitate the hermetic structure of Mallarmé. "Parce que strictement de par le double fer" is a pastiche of Mallarmé where by the use of striking verse rhymes (dresse-Arès), and a structure based on long, unique sentences, there is a tendency to make things hermetic. The poem, however, does not seem to have any sense at all, except some erotic allusions out of which one may conclude a defeat of viril dignity by a sadistic woman:

> Parce que strictement de par le double fer
> Le deuil bref aplani d'aspect viril se dresse,
> Parce que sur la ride où vit l'ardeur d'Arès
> Une ombre en linéaments rares se profère,
>
> Et qu'aussi la stature et le geste d'avoir
> Et si peu d'aurore ambiguë, émaciée,
> Disent au Récitant l'imaginaire acier
> Dont la garde enracine un jeune dieu d'ivoire,
>
> Il me plaît, comme aussi l'opposé conquérir
> Le caprice animal d'attendre et de sourire
> Où subjugue une intervertie aux doigts rétifs,
>
> Le héros, grave de sa fureur qui s'ennuie,
> En navrant, symétrique et protecteur, la nuit
> Cyclopéenne au fond des parts rétrospectives. [40]

---

[39] Ibid., p. 247.

[40] Louÿs, Oeuvres, I, p. 190.

André Fontainas' sonnet "Offrande," read at
Valvins in 1936 is a real hommage to Mallarmé. The
pastiche consists in allusions, quotes, and the sketching of the contents of the poems of Mallarmé, for
example, "...la Reine farouche" of the second tercet
referring to "Hérodiade."

Le visage et la voix se nouent en filigrane
Flexible comme un lys ou frappé d'un rehaut
Quand s'avive au vélin comme elle sans défaut,
MAITRE, une âme, la vôtre, intacte et diaphane.

Quel songe suscité par votre nom, Stéphane
Mallarmé ne flamboie et n'embaume, sursaut
A jamais triomphal, un jardin où prévaut
Le fixe éclat de "fleurs dont nulle ne se fane"?

Simple, ici vous viviez, Forêt, fleuve, le seuil,
L'escalier verdissant, l'émoi de votre accueil:
Vous étiez pur et bon...Musicienne, une aile

Frôlait le vierge espace et dressait dans le soir
Le Faune dont la flûte en chants d'éclairs ruisselle
Et la Reine farouche offerte à son miroir. [41]

The pastiche of Mallarmé by the minor Symbolists
was not widespread. Only a few fervent followers attempted
his patterns, and with few exceptions they throw little
light on the original. There are, of course, echoes
of Mallarmé in the works of the minor poets, and we
have tried to indicate them throughout this dissertation.
The full pastiche, however, is rare, and limited to
such poets as Fontainas and Louÿs, whose original poems
in the manner of Mallarmé often illuminate, as much as
their mannered imitations indicated here and in the
last section, the original poems of Mallarmé.

----

[41]Fontainas, Choix, p. 218.

CONCLUSION

Our investigation has shown that the majority
of the minor Symbolists are not disciples of Mallarmé.
All of the poets show sporadic attempts at imitation,
but few of them are able to achieve his type of poetry.
What they did was approach Mallarmé's poetic form
either through content and/or exterior devices which
while aiming in the right direction, did not equal the
master example. Our fundamental assumption, in harmony
with the overwhelming majority of contemporary critics,
is that Mallarmé's type of poetry represents the ideal
of poésie pure.

A common trait of Mallarmé and the minor poets
is a subject matter which is similar, at least in its
most elementary purpose. Since the time of the Romantics, angoisse has been a characteristic cry of the
poets, and all of the Symbolists are joined in a
common chant of frustration and incompletion, but on
different levels.

A common denominator can be noted in Symbolist
imagery. There is a penchant on all side from Mallarmé
down for ideal paysages, for pastoral, mythical, legendary, and medieval landscapes, in particular for swans,
fauns, nymphs, ladies in mourning. Also is found an
artificial-cultural-object imagery, vases, rooms, pre-
cious stones, flowers, and so on. A specific study
might reveal a Symbolism which could be united on the
basis of its imagery, which works within certain restricted
areas. Here Mallarmé utilizes for his own purposes an
imagery which is being exploited by others at the same
time. All evidence points to the conclusion that Mallarmé's "Après-Midi d'un Faune," "Hérodiade," and at
least "Le Vierge, le vivace, et le bel aujourd'hui"
are responsible for an increased diffusion of faun,
virgin, and swan images which are found in all the poets
in the last ten years of the century. A significant

136

intrusion of Mallarméan vocabulary would be equally
discernible. All of this, however, is conjecture
based mostly on passing observations.

Real approximation of Mallarmé, as we have
pointed out in the text, is to be found in the Symbolist
drive toward idealism and synthetic expression. On
both of these points again the minor Symbolists are not
able to measure up to the Mallarméan standard.

Unified expression was achieved by the minor
Symbolists through a determined and widespread use of
traditional poetic forms. This means that the Symbolists
mainly succeeded in developing and expanding the lyricism reborn at the beginning of the century, until it
had achieved at least a partial degree of transformation into symbol. The progress was from discursive
to hermetic structure. Lyricism combined with an increased use of a popular type of poetry, in the frequent use of repetition and refrain as unifying devices.
Allegory and personification were transformed by their
lyric quality, abstract allegories tended to disappear
and to be replaced by the modern allegory of things.
For most of the minor Symbolists, the successful use
of such devices was the maximum achievement in the
direction of synthesis.

This evidence alone allows us to attempt a
definition of Symbolism. We would concur with the
opinion of many scholars and critics who wrote that
the movement may not be considered as a unified school
of poets. Rather there are common traits and unifying
bonds among them all which can best be expressed by the
word Symbolist for lack of a better one. Strictly observed, the term can only be applied to Mallarmé and
a few other major poets. Used freely to describe the
poetic renaissance at the end of the nineteenth century,
it must only mean the anguish and the idealism of the
late nineteenth century writers who sought to seek or
create a spiritual world from poetry, in which they
could escape from their growing dissatisfaction with
a materialistic society. From this situation poetry
assumed new importance, took on metaphysical propor-
tions, and became, so to speak, an absolute existence.

The new belief in a poetic existence, in a world beyond experience, gave rise to urgent needs for unity
and synthesis. Many poetic theories were formulated,
all of which converged toward the same point, the _vers
libre_ of Kahn, the _école instrumentale verbale_ of
Ghil, the motif symbolism of Mallarmé. The work of
Mallarmé -and this can be stated on the basis of analysis and comparison- represents the top achievement
in synthesis, the greatest poetic reduction possible.
Such is the atmosphere in general of Symbolism, and

he writes:

> Nul poète n'a dédaigné, avec plus de
> hauteur, moins de retard, et sans au-
> cune recherche d'impassibilité ou d'-
> inhumanité, l'utilisation littéraire
> des caprices de sa vie et des effusions
> de la douleur personnelle.[1]

The discipline of Mallarmé as contrasted with the free-
dom of lyrical expression is well-expressed by Jean-
Paul Zimmermann when he contrasts Mallarméan concentration with Surrealistic expansion. In the final
analysis I think it not highly improbable that a goodly
portion of the surrealist effort may be interpreted
in terms of a modern lyricism, and it is for this
reason that the remarks of Zimmermann seem to describe
the discrepancy between Mallarmé and the minor poets:

> Les autres sont toute éruption, toute
> expansion, ils s'exaltent des limites
> outrepassées, renversées, des trouées
> fulgurantes ouvertes dans les défenses
> jalouses des horizons, des visions et
> des mirages suscités dans les lointains
> fabuleux du songe, ils instituent le dé-
> règlement systematique de tous les sens,
> ils réinventent la ville, la faim, l'amour,
> le bruit. Son progrès à lui n'est que de
> concentration, il plonge en lui-même, il
> tend vers ce point idéal où, du monde
> spirituel et de la pensée attentive qui
> compose les pures essences et en perçoit
> les rapports, se recueille en millions de
> feux, hors de toute dimension et de toute
> durée, le glorieux anéantissement. [2]

---

[1] Henri Mondor, *Vie de Mallarme*, I (Paris, 1941),
p. 71.

[2] Jean-Paul Zimmermann in *Stéphane Mallarmé,
Essais et témoignages* (Neuchâtel, 1942), p. 21.

Herein can be found the necessary distinctions between
Mallarmé and his less illustrious imitators. Mallarmé
is especially a metaphysical poet who worked toward a
purification of his work. This means that poetry had
to undergo an internal metamorphosis which would strip
the poetic creation of aesthetically impure material,
in order to keep out non-poetic matter (experience
vécue, sensation, emotion). Mallarmé conceived of
the analogy in the sense attributed to it by Fiser
when he states that:

> C'est donc l'analogie qui donne aux objets
> inanimés un sens spirituel et, par là, artis-
> tique. Sans cette spiritualisation, sans
> cette transformation de la matière brute en
> matière spirituelle il n'y aurait pas
> d'expression métaphorique possible.[3]

He consequently worked toward the creation of a poetry
where form and content would be so joined as to be inseparable, the form in the content and the content in
the form. The hermetic creations of Mallarmé are explained by the fact that only through a shrewd manipulation of language could thought, which is derived
from a reasoned reshuffling of experience, be eliminated, and an autonomous poetic actuality be brought
about. Mallarmé is not an obscure poet in the sense
that the hermetic poem is only hiding a discernible
reality. Rather his hermetic constructions, if taken
seriously, are profound in that they reveal a hitherto
non-discovered reality. For this reason when Pierre
Jean Jouve writes that "La creation de Mallarmé est
verbale-ce qui veut dire qu'elle est à l'opposé du
verbalisme. Une création verbale est une création
métaphysique." [4] he underlines the fundamental difference

---

[3]E. Fiser, Le Symbole littéraire (Paris, n.d.),
p. 135. [4]Pierre Jean Jouve in Stéphane Mallarmé, Essais
et témoignages, pp. 29-30.

between Mallarmé and the minor Symbolists, Mallarmé
and the Surrealists, and even Mallarmé and Valéry.
There is a discernible ratio between the Mallarméan
creation and an innate lyricism. A comparison of
Symbolist poets from the viewpoint of purpose of evocation as it is revealed in the structure and images
of the poems, shows the minor Symbolists floundering
in a realm between the lyric and the infra-lyric or
supra-lyric. This corresponds in actuality with an
historical development.

    If we were to concentrate on one common
Symbolist figure, the swan, we would have to conclude
that the minor Symbolist achievement in its best instances
locates itself between the swan of Baudelaire and the
swan of Mallarmé. A comparison of the voyage poems to
the ideal land would reveal the same situation, "Prose
pour des Esseintes" being the supreme achievement,
followed by all sorts of symbolist mixtures: the many
embarkments for Cythera where corrupt and decadent
human emotions are veiled in a refined sensibility
(Verlaine, Samain, Mikhaël, Merrill, De Régnier), the
allegorical lands in which human love and the poetic
ideal flower side by side (Fontainas, De Régnier, Mikhaël) are indicative of the mélange found in the minor
writers. This means that the image is often a lyric
decoration, a substitution for the symbol. It often
means expressing the mysteries of life by creating an
atmosphere of dream and mystery (the sleeping swan re-
places the frozen swan). The idealism of the minor
poets is primarily earthbound despite its pretentions
to new spiritual realms and its quasi-symbolic success.
The minor poets are caught between the real and the
ideal with the ideal often only camouflaging the real.

Maritain points this out when he writes:

> The creative emotion of minor poets
> is born in a flimsy twilight and at
> a comparatively superficial level in

> the soul. Great poets descend into
> the creative night and touch the deep
> waters over which it reigns. Poets
> of genius have their dwelling place in
> this night and never leave the shores
> of these deep waters.[5]

This in general indicates the position of the minor
French Symbolist poets. A gradation exists in which a
depth process is discernible, and the whole process of
deep lyrical allegory and unified imagery indicative
of the idealism of the times cannot be dismissed as a
latent romanticism. To the contrary, we have tried to
show exactly what are the symbolic manifestations within these works. We would only insist on the recogni-
tion of an underlying lyricism, and ultimately, depend-
ing on the viewpoint, the question may be asked even of
Mallarmé. How lyrical, how earthbound is Hérodiade?
The discovery of allegorical and mannered
descriptions veiled in a hermetic structure brings out
another aspect of the same problem. Hermetic structure
is not indicative of new meaning unless there is an
interior transformation at the same time. We have
noted in numerous examples that an actual motif symbolism, brought about through autonomous and ambiguous
images has been produced in many poems by Raynaud,
De Régnier, Fontainas, Louÿs and Royère. They are
truly disciples of Mallarmé at least in the poems
we chose for analysis. We discovered at the same time,
however, that in an equal number of instances, these
poets were also expressing ordinary lyric emotion in
the sense of the discursive poets. Herein lies one of
the fundamental problems of Poésie pure which has been
discussed in some quarters with a subsequent clarifi-
cation.

---

[5]Maritain, Creative Intuition, pp. 372-373.

There is first of all too great a readiness
to see modern poetry universally on the march toward
a new spiritual realm as a means to another end than
poetry itself. Daniel-Rops remarks that it is a
common tendency today to equate poetry and mysticism,
to see in the common non-discursive traits of poetry
a secular experience comparable to the experience of
the mystic.[6] Unfortunately he stops short of the
possible real parallelism between the two "gropings
in darkness", one ending in Divine Union, the other
in artistic creation. On this point which one may
accept or reject, at least Bremond, Jacques and
Raïssa Maritain are in full agreement. A close study
of text, however, will not sustain the so called mystical bent of all modern poets. An examination less
of what the poet says and more of what he accomplishes
will reveal that distinctions can be made between the
poets, necessary distinctions for any resolution of
the problem of poésie pure. What is the difference
between the poems which we have classified as motif
symbol poems, and those poems which we have called
mannered? If they can be differentiated, then perhaps we can somewhat define poésie pure. In the analysis of the motif symbol poems, the image could not be
restricted to one meaning, and in quality it was in-
tangible and elusive. In such cases, the image had
been transformed, it had been reduced to an essence
from which all the particulars could emanate. The
mannered poems, on the other hand, showed a clever
manipulation of language, and a difficult, but not
transformed imagery. In the mannered descriptive
poems, an actual vision with precise limitations could
be grasped. In the allegories, the image could be
seen as coming from thought and limiting itself to a
philosophical explanation of the universe.

---

[6]Henry Daniel-Rops, Où Passent des anges
(Paris, 1947), p. 227.

The situation existing between Mallarmé and the minor Symbolists who copied his style is the same which exists in many instances between Mallarmé and Valéry, as Johansen has aptly shown. Valéry is allegedly a great poet, and a great Symbolist poet, as may be proved particularly by sections of La Jeune Parque. Quite frequently, however, his images are based on thought. Like the minor Symbolist mannerists, Valéry is more engaged in the battle of the flesh and the spirit than perhaps his own abstract mind would like to believe. This distinction is made clear by Helmut Hatzfeld in his recent literary study on Valéry and St. John of the Cross.[7] In a chapter entitled "Paul Valéry descubre a San Juan de la Cruz," the author makes a comparison of the works of Valéry and San Juan with the view of elucidating the problem of poésie pure. A comparison of San Juan's "En una noche oscura" with Valéry's "Les Pas" clarifies a basic issue, and shows that there is perhaps a closer affiliation between Mallarmé and San Juan than between Valéry and Mallarmé. The principal image in both poems works out of a real, lyric, earthly love situation. In the poem of San Juan, the soul in search of the Divine Lover is like a girl going out of the house of her parents in search of the loved one; Inspiration coming to the poet, an analogous situation, is compared in Valéry's poem to the mistress coming to the bed of her lover. Pure poetry demands that the image in both cases be transformed, purified, or else a lyric and not a symbol will result. Such is not the case in the poem of Valéry where the allegorical element remains high because the sensual nature of the image predominates:

---

[7]Helmut Hatzfeld, Estudios literarios sobre Mística espanola (Madrid, 1955).

Las imágenes en cuanto tales guardan en ambos
íntima relacion: una muchacha enamorada que
camina en el silencio de la noche a encontrar
al amado. El poeta español es mucho mas explícito
en cuanto a las implicaciones amorosas; a pesar
de ello, nos sentimos ante una amante casi incor-
poral que permanece invisible, perdo adivinamos
su feliz rubor de enamorada segura de sí misma.
No se oye más que su voz que se alza en alabanza
de su noche de bodas, para la que se ufana de
haber conservado puro su florido pecho. El poeta
francés, por su parte, se ve obligado a llamar a
su Musa, como una mujer amada, 'pure créature'
que se acerca 'santamente' a su 'lecho' mientras
el la está esperando. Además se hace a uno
difícil creer en su santidad y no cuesta mucho
trabajo identificar en la oscuridad esta criatura
'divina', pero no exactamente novia, a la que se
aplican los calificativos de 'silente', 'fria',
y 'dulce' y de quien se dice que viene 'descalza'
y 'con labios tendidos' buscando 'la limosna de
un beso'. De la poesía 'doblemente' pura de
San Juan de la Cruz se desprende una limpia
catarsis, de la poesia pseudopura de Valéry una
turbia sensación. 8

    Although Hatzfeld tries to make a point of
the identity of moral and aesthetic purity in literature, we are stressing here only the one side of the
problem, the aesthetic and not the moral purity. The
same situation is to be seen in the non-motif hermetic
poems which we have discussed in this paper. Poésie
pure is very difficult to attain and sustain. Among
the French Symbolists, only Mallarmé was able to do
this, and with Igitur he seems to have reached the
end possibility. Most of the poets never attain it,

8Ibid., p. 394.

and remain restricted to a discursive lyric. Some
poets, De Régnier, Fontainas, Louÿs, Royère, and on
a more artistic level, Valéry sometimes achieve the
motif, at other times fall back into allegorical and
lyrical patterns which are expressed in the new hermetic structure. Poetry at the end of the nineteenth
century vacillates between the lyric and the supra-
lyric. This does not mean that such poetry is not
original and modern. Rather it is a commentary on
the actual human condition, the paradox of man torn
between the physical and the spiritual. Perhaps
poésie pure is a rare atmosphere which is prohibited
by the very condition humaine of the writers. How
possible is the complete sacrifice of the human personality? This is pointed out by Marc Eigeldinger
when he writes:

> C'est à bon droit que l'on peut objecter à une
> défense de l'angélisme la catastrophe d'Igitur,
> le silence de Rimbaud ou l'échec du surréalisme,
> mais ne convient-il pas parfois de considérer
> un résultat comme provisoire, une issue comme
> momentanée, surtout lorsqu'il s'agit d'un art
> tel que la poésie qui recèle mille secrètes
> possibilités et dont la destinée peut rester
> en suspens. Le poète extrait de la conscience
> de sa défaite une poignante incantation, il
> puise en elle la substance même de son message
> ....Le thème de la brèche, de la catastrophe
> est latent dans toute la poésie contemporaine,
> il lui est étroitement associé parce qu'il se
> confond avec l'aboutissement de ses recherches.
> Le démon de la poésie moderne est de hanter
> l'irréel et de tenter ce qu'elle sait l'impossible.[9]

---

[9] Marc Eigeldinger, Poésie et tendances
(Neuchâtel, 1945), pp. 38-39.

Thus it may be that the effort of Mallarmé was singular and unique in French letters. He has many followers, but necessarily only a few imitators. The fact that in most cases he is not imitated does not minimize his presence. He increased the spiritual awareness of the minor writers, and pointed to a non-material ideal. He is the leading example showing the way from discursive prose-like poetry to the purer poetry of today. His actual imitation can be seen in a small but respectable number of poems of which we have given the most convincing examples.

Ultimately his influence can be decided in terms of the direction he gave to poetry after him. The fifty odd years since his death seem to indicate that a poetry which is discursive is not regarded as poetry at all. His direct influence on contemporary poets would be difficult to prove. General rapports between his work and that of the modern poets like Saint-John Perse, for example, can be made, and they show some striking similarities, particularly of symbolic, hermetic aloofness.[10]

Symbolism of the 1890's was poetry in transition, caught between the old and the new. That Mallarmé shaped to a great extent the minor poets, capable or not of imitating him, has been the contention of this dissertation. This was seen in their definite transformation of lyricism, and in their more or less perfect, that is at least exterior imitation of the actual technique of the motif symbol.

---

[10]See Arthur J. Knodel, "The Imagery of Saint-John Perse's Neiges," PMLA, LXX (March, 1955), pp. 5-18.

BIBLIOGRAPHY

Poems

Baudelaire, Charles. *Les Fleurs du mal*. Paris:
    Bibliothèque de Cluny, 1938.

Elskamp, Max. *Enluminures*. Brussels: Paul Lacomblez,
    1898.

_____. *La Louange de la vie*. Paris: Mercure
    de France, 1898.

Fontainas, André. *Choix de poèmes*. Paris: Mercure
    de France, 1950.

_____. *Le sang des fleurs*. Brussels:
    Veuve Monnom, 1889.

Ghil, René. *Oeuvres complètes*. 3 vols. Paris:
    Albert Messein, 1938.

Gide, André. *Poésie, Journal, Souvenirs*. Vol. I.
    Paris: Gallimard, 1952.

_____. *Le Voyage d'Urien*. Paris: Gallimard,
    1929.

Kahn, Gustave. *La Pluie et le beau temps*. Paris:
    Vanier, 1896.

_____. *Le Livre d'images*. 2nd ed. Paris:
    Mercure de France, 1897.

_____. *Premiers poèmes*. 2nd ed. Paris:
    Mercure de France, 1897.

148

La Tailhède, Raymond de. Les Poésies de Raymond de La Tailhède. Paris: Albin Michel, 1938.

Le Cardonnel, Louis. Poèmes. 6th ed. Paris: Mercure de France, 1904.

Louÿs, Pierre. Les Poèmes de Pierre Louÿs 1887-1924. 2 vols. Edited by Yves-Gérard le Dantec. Paris: Albin Michel, 1945.

Maeterlinck, Maurice. Serres chaudes. Brussels: Paul Lacomblez, 1900.

Mallarmé, Stéphane. Oeuvres complètes. Text established and annotated by Henri Mondor and G. Jean-Aubry. Paris: Gallimard, 1951.

Mauclair, Camille. Sonatines d'automne. Paris: Librarie Académique Didier, Perrin, 1895.

Merrill, Stuart. Les quatre saisons. 2nd ed. Paris: Mercure de France, 1900.

_____. Poèmes 1887-1897. Paris: Mercure de France, 1897.

Mikhaël, Ephraïm. Oeuvres de Ephraïm Mikhaël. Paris: Lemerre, 1890.

Mockel, Albert. Clartés. Paris: Mercure de France, 1901.

_____. La Flamme immortelle. Paris: La Renaissance du Livre, 1924.

Moréas, Jean. Oeuvres de Jean Moréas. Vols. I, II. Paris: Mercure de France, 1923.

Quillard, Pierre. La Lyre héroïque et dolente. Paris: Mercure de France, 1897.

150

Raynaud, Ernest. La Couronne des jours. Paris:
Mercure de France, 1905.

_____. Le Bocage. Paris: Bibliothèque
Artistique et Littéraire, 1895.

_____. Les Cornes du faune. Paris:
Bibliothèque Artistique et Littéraire, 1890.

Régnier, Henri de. Les Jeux rustiques et divins.
16th ed. Paris: Mercure de France, 1921.

_____. Poèmes 1887-1892. Paris: Mercure
de France, 1897.

_____. Premiers poèmes. Paris: Mercure
de France, 1898.

Rodenbach, Georges. Bruges-La-Morte. 8th ed. Paris:
Flammarion, n.d.

_____. Oeuvres de Georges Rodenbach.
Vols. I, II. Paris: Mercure de France, 1923,
1925.

Royère, Jean. Exil doré. Paris: Vanier, 1898.

_____. Poésies. Amiens: Malfère, 1924.

Samain, Albert. Le Chariot d'or. Paris: Mercure de
France, 1947.

_____. Au Jardin de l'Infante. Paris:
Mercure de France, 1947.

Van Bever, Ad. and Paul Léautaud. Poètes d'aujourd'hui.
2 vols. Paris: Mercure de France, 1927.

Verhaeren, Emile. Choix de poèmes. Paris: Mercure
de France, 1948.

Verlaine, Paul. *Choix de poésies*. Paris: Charpentier, 1948.

Vielé-Griffin, Francis. *Oeuvres de Francis Vielé-Griffin*. 3 vols. Paris: Mercure de France, 1924, 1926, 1927.

References

Aish, Deborah Amelia Kirk. *La métaphore dans l'oeuvre de Stéphane Mallarmé*. Paris: Droz, 1938.

Baju, Anatole. *L'Ecole décadente*. Paris: Vanier, 1887.

Balakian, Anna Elizabeth. *Literary Origins of Surrealism*. New York: King's Crown Press, 1947.

Beausire, Pierre. *Mallarmé, poésie et poétique*. Mermod, 1949.

Bellot, Etienne. *Notes sur le Symbolisme*. Paris: Linard, 1908.

Bonneau, Georges. *Le Symbolisme dans la poésie française contemporaine*. Paris: Bowin, 1930.

Bornecque, Jacques Henri. "Rêves et réalités du Symbolisme," *Revue des sciences humaines*, No. 77 (1955), 5-23.

Bremond, Henri. *La Poésie pure*. Paris: Grasset, 1926.

Chiari, Joseph. *Contemporary French Poetry*. Manchester: Manchester University Press, 1952.

Clancier, Georges. De Rimbaud au Surréalisme. Paris:
        Pierre Seghers, 1953.

Coulon, Marcel. Témoignages. 3rd series. Paris:
        Mercure de France, 1913.

Cours, Jean de. Francis Vielé-Griffin, son oeuvre,
        sa pensée, son art. Paris, 1930.

Daniel-Rops, Henry. Notre inquiétude. 3rd ed. Paris:
        Perrin, 1927.

_____. Où Passent des anges. Paris:
        Plon, 1947.

Delfel, Guy. L'Esthétique de Mallarmé. Paris:
        Flammarion, 1951.

Dérieux, Henry. La Poésie française contemporaine
        1885-1935. Paris: Mercure de France, 1935.

Dinar, André. La Croisade symboliste. Paris: Mercure
        de France, 1943.

Eigeldinger, Marc. L'Evolution dynamique de l'image.
        Neuchâtel: André Seiler et Fils, 1943.

_____. Poésie et tendances. Neuchâtel:
        A La Baconnière, 1945.

Fiser, E. Le Symbole littéraire. Paris: José Corti,
        1941.

Fontainas, André. Confession d'un poète. Paris:
        Mercure de France, 1936.

_____. Dans la lignée de Baudelaire.
        Paris: Editions de la Nouvelle Revue Critique,
        1930.

_____. *Tableau de la poésie française d'aujourd'hui*. Paris: Editions de la Nouvelle Revue Critique, 1931.

Fort, Paul, and Louis Mandin. *Histoire de la poésie française depuis 1850*. Paris, 1926.

Fowlie, Wallace. *Jacob's Night*. New York: Sheed and Ward, 1947.

_____. *Mallarmé*. Chicago: The University of Chicago Press, 1953.

Gengoux, Jacques. *Le Symbolisme de Mallarmé*. Paris: Nizet, 1950.

_____. "Le Symbolisme et les Symbolismes," *Les Lettres Romanes*, V, no. 1 (February, 1951), 3-37.

Ghil, René. *Les Dates et les oeuvres*. Paris: Crès, 1923.

Gourmont, Remy de. *Le Deuxième Livre des masques*. 5th ed. Paris: Mercure de France, 1910.

_____. *Le Livre des masques*. 7th ed. Paris: Mercure de France, 1914.

Guiraud, Pierre. *Index du vocabulaire du Symbolisme*. Vol. III, *Index des mots des poésies de Stéphane Mallarmé*. Paris: C. Klincksieck, 1953.

Hatzfeld, Helmut. *Estudios literarios sobre Mística española*. Madrid: Gredos, 1955.

_____. *Literature Through Art*. New York: Oxford University Press, 1952.

Henry, Marjorie Louise. La Contribution d'un Américain
  au symbolisme français. Paris: Champion, 1927.

Huret, Jules. Enquête sur l'évolution littéraire.
  Paris: Charpentier, 1913.

Johansen, Svend. Le Symbolisme. Copenhagen:
  Munksgaard, 1945.

Kahn, Gustave. Les Origines du symbolisme. Paris:
  Messein, 1936.

Knodel, Arthur J. "The Imagery of Saint-John Perse's
  Neiges," PMLA, LXX, no. 1 (March, 1955), 5-18.

Krafft, Jacques. La Forme et l'idée en poésie. Paris:
  Vrin, 1944.

Laforgue, Jules. Choix de poésies. New York: Bren-
  tano, n.d.

Maritain, Jacques. Creative Intuition in Art and
  Poetry. New York: Pantheon Books, 1953.

Mazel, Henri. Aux beaux temps du symbolisme 1890-
  1895. Paris: Mercure de France, 1943.

Mendès, Catulle. Le Mouvement poétique français de
  1867 à 1900. Paris: Imprimerie nationale, 1903.

Merrill, Stuart. "Souvenirs sur le symbolisme," La
  Plume, (December 15, 1903).

Mockel, Albert. Stéphane Mallarmé un héros. Paris:
  Mercure de France, 1899.

Mondor, Henri. Vie de Mallarmé. 2 vols. 10th ed.
  Paris: Gallimard, 1941, 1942.

Noulet, Emilie. Dix Poèmes de Mallarmé. Geneva:
Droz, 1948.

——————. L'Oeuvre poétique de Mallarmé. Paris:
Droz, 1940.

Piérard, Louis. Un Poète de la vie populaire: Max
Elskamp. Brussels: Van Oest, 1915.

Raymond, Marcel. De Baudelaire au Surréalisme.
Paris: José Corti, 1947.

Régnier, Henri de. Faces et profils. Paris: Jacques
Bernard, 1931.

Réverdy, Pierre. "La Fonction poétique," Mercure de
France, Vol. 308, (1950), 584-592.

Revue Wagnérienne. Vols. I, II, III. Paris: 1886-1888.

Rousseaux, André, "Le Mythe de Narcisse dans le symbolisme," in his Le Monde classique. Paris:
Albin Michel, 1946, 227-232.

Royère, Jean. Mallarmé. Paris: Albert Messein, 1931.

Scherer, Jacques. L'Expression littéraire dans l'oeuvre
de Mallarmé. Paris: Droz, 1947.

Stéphane Mallarmé, Essais et témoignages. Neuchâtel:
A La Baconnière, 1942.

Stevens, Wallace. The Necessary Angel. New York:
Alfred A. Knopf, 1951.

Thibaudet, Albert. La Poésie de Mallarmé. 5th ed. Paris:
Nouvelle Revue Française, 1929.

Vigée, Claude. "Metamorphoses of Modern Poetry," Com-
parative Literature, VII, no. 2 (1955), 97-120.

INDEX